Henri de Toulouse-Lautrec

GREAT ACHIEVERS

LIVES OF THE PHYSICALLY CHALLENGED

Henri de Toulouse-Lautrec

ARTIST

Jennifer Fisher Bryant

Chelsea House Publishers

New York • Philadelphia

CHELSEA HOUSE PUBLISHERS

EDITORIAL DIRECTOR   Richard Rennert
EXECUTIVE MANAGING EDITOR   Karyn Gullen Browne
COPY CHIEF   Robin James
PICTURE EDITOR   Adrian G. Allen
ART DIRECTOR   Robert Mitchell
MANUFACTURING DIRECTOR   Gerald Levine
ASSISTANT ART DIRECTOR   Joan Ferrigno

GREAT ACHIEVERS: LIVES OF THE PHYSICALLY CHALLENGED

SENIOR EDITOR   Kathy Kuhtz Campbell
SERIES DESIGN   Basia Niemczyc

Staff for HENRI DE TOULOUSE-LAUTREC

ASSISTANT EDITOR   Joy Sanchez
COPY EDITOR   Catherine Iannone
EDITORIAL ASSISTANT   Scott D. Briggs
PICTURE RESEARCHER   Pat Burns
COVER ILLUSTRATION   Alex Zwarenstein

First Printing

1   3   5   7   9   8   6   4   2

Library of Congress Cataloging-in-Publication Data

Bryant, Jennifer.
Henri de Toulouse-Lautrec, artist / Jennifer Fisher Bryant.
p. cm.—(Great achievers)
Includes bibliographical references and index.
ISBN 0-7910-2408-3
       0-7910-2409-1 (pbk.)
1. Toulouse-Lautrec, Henri de, 1864–1901—Juvenile literature. 2. Artists—
France—Biography—Juvenile literature. 3. Physically handicapped painters—
France—Biography—Juvenile literature. [1. Toulouse-Lautrec, Henri de,
1864–1901. 2. Artists. 3. Physically handicapped.] I. Title. II. Series:
Great achievers (Chelsea House Publishers)
ND553.T7B78 1994   94-17327
760'.092—dc20   CIP

FRONTISPIECE:

Henri de Toulouse-Lautrec painted this self-portrait, looking in a mirror, in 1880. The painting today hangs in the Toulouse-Lautrec Museum in Albi, France.

CONTENTS

GREAT ACHIEVERS

LIVES OF THE PHYSICALLY CHALLENGED

A MESSAGE FOR EVERYONE

Jerry Lewis

Just 44 years ago—when I was the ripe old age of 23—an incredible stroke of fate rocketed me to overnight stardom as an entertainer. After the initial shock wore off, I began to have a very strong feeling that, in return for all life had given me, I must find a way of giving something back. At just that moment, a deeply moving experience in my personal life persuaded me to take up the leadership of a fledgling battle to defeat a then little-known group of diseases called muscular dystrophy, as well as other related neuromuscular diseases—all of which are disabling and, in the worst cases, cut life short.

In 1950, when the Muscular Dystrophy Association (MDA)—of which I am national chairman—was established, physical disability was looked on as a matter of shame. Franklin Roosevelt, who guided America through World War II from a wheelchair, and Harold Russell, the World War II hero who lost both hands in battle, then became an Academy Award–winning movie star and chairman of the President's Committee on Employment of the Handicapped, were the exceptions. One of the reasons that muscular dystrophy and related diseases were so little known was that people who had been disabled by them were hidden at home, away from the pity and discomfort with which they were generally regarded by society. As I got to know and began working with people who have disabilities, I quickly learned what a tragic mistake this perception was. And my determination to correct this terrible problem

7

soon became as great as my commitment to see disabling neuromuscular diseases wiped from the face of the earth.

I have long wondered why it never occurs to us, as we experience the knee-jerk inclination to feel sorry for people who are physically disabled, that lives such as those led by President Roosevelt, Harold Russell, and all of the extraordinary people profiled in this Great Achievers series demonstrate unmistakably how wrong we are. Physical disability need not be something that blights life and destroys opportunity for personal fulfillment and accomplishment. On the contrary, as people such as Ray Charles, Stephen Hawking, and Ron Kovic prove, physical disability can be a spur to greatness rather than a condemnation of emptiness.

In fact, if my experience with physically disabled people can be taken as a guide, as far as accomplishment is concerned, they have a slight edge on the rest of us. The unusual challenges they face require finding greater-than-average sources of energy and determination to achieve much of what able-bodied people take for granted. Often, this ultimately translates into a lifetime of superior performance in whatever endeavor people with disabilities choose to pursue.

If you have watched my Labor Day Telethon over the years, you know exactly what I am talking about. Annually, we introduce to tens of millions of Americans people whose accomplishments would distinguish them regardless of their physical conditions—top-ranking executives, physicians, scientists, lawyers, musicians, and artists. The message I hope the audience receives is not that these extraordinary individuals have achieved what they have by overcoming a dreadful disadvantage that the rest of us are lucky not to have to endure. Rather, I hope our viewers reflect on the fact that these outstanding people have been ennobled and strengthened by the tremendous challenges they have faced.

In 1992, MDA, which has grown over the past four decades into one of the world's leading voluntary health agencies, established a personal achievement awards program to demonstrate to the nation that the distinctive qualities of people with disabilities are by no means confined to the famous. What could have been more appropriate or timely in that year of the implementation of the 1990 Americans with Disabilities Act than to take an action that could perhaps finally achieve the alteration of public perception of disability, which MDA had struggled over four decades to achieve?

On Labor Day, 1992, it was my privilege to introduce to America MDA's inaugural national personal achievement award winner, Steve Mikita, assistant attorney general of the state of Utah. Steve graduated magna cum laude from Duke University as its first wheelchair student in history and was subsequently named the outstanding young lawyer of the year by the Utah Bar Association. After he spoke on the Telethon with an eloquence that caused phones to light up from coast to coast, people asked me where he had been all this time and why they had not known of him before, so deeply impressed were they by him. I answered that he and thousands like him have been here all along. We just have not adequately *noticed* them.

It is my fervent hope that we can eliminate indifference once and for all and make it possible for all of our fellow citizens with disabilities to gain their rightfully high place in our society.

ON FACING CHALLENGES

John Callahan

I was paralyzed for life in 1972, at the age of 21. A friend and I were driving in a Volkswagen on a hot July night, when he smashed the car at full speed into a utility pole. He suffered only minor injuries. But my spinal cord was severed during the crash, leaving me without any feeling from my diaphragm downward. The only muscles I could move were some in my upper body and arms, and I could also extend my fingers. After spending a lot of time in physical therapy, it became possible for me to grasp a pen.

I've always loved to draw. When I was a kid, I made pictures of everything from Daffy Duck (one of my lifelong role models) to caricatures of my teachers and friends. I've always been a people watcher, it seems; and I've always looked at the world in a sort of skewed way. Everything I see just happens to translate immediately into humor. And so, humor has become my way of coping. As the years have gone by, I have developed a tremendous drive to express my humor by drawing cartoons.

The key to cartooning is to put a different spin on the expected, the normal. And that's one reason why many of my cartoons deal with the disabled: amputees, quadriplegics, paraplegics, the blind. The public is not used to seeing them in cartoons.

But there's another reason why my subjects are often disabled men and women. I'm sick and tired of people who presume to speak for the disabled. Call me a cripple, call me a gimp, call me paralyzed for life.

Just don't call me something I'm not. I'm not "differently abled," and my cartoons show that disabled people should not be treated any differently than anyone else.

All of the men, women, and children who are profiled in the Great Achievers series share this in common: their various handicaps have not prevented them from accomplishing great things. Their life stories are worth knowing about because they have found the strength and courage to develop their talents and to follow their dreams as fully as they can.

Whether able-bodied or disabled, a person must strive to overcome obstacles. There's nothing greater than to see a person who faces challenges and conquers them, regardless of his or her limitations.

*French artist Lautrec stood only five feet tall as an adult. His torso
was of normal size, but his legs stopped growing after he suffered
two falls when he was young, the result of an incurable bone disease.
This photograph was taken in 1892 when he was 27 years old.*

1

A Golden Opportunity

ON A WARM SPRING NIGHT IN 1891, a horse-drawn taxi slowed to a stop at the corner of rue Lepic and la place Blanche in Paris, France. The sole passenger stepped carefully down from the backseat and onto the sidewalk, paid the driver, and turned toward the doorway below the spinning red windmill. The gaslit street lamps, which cast a soft glow on the cobblestones, revealed a small, well-dressed man of no more than five feet tall, wearing a tweed jacket, silk tie, and felt hat. A thick, black beard partially concealed his large yet friendly face, which was dominated by a pair of dark, twinkling eyes.

"Bonsoir, Monsieur Lautrec!" announced Joseph Oller, one of the owners of the Moulin Rouge (Red Mill), as the passenger approached the nightclub's entrance. Henri de Toulouse-Lautrec acknowledged the greeting with a slight tip of his hat and proceeded down the hallway leading to the main room of the dance hall. More friendly greetings followed, for Lautrec was a regular patron and was well known among the employees and the performers. As always, there were a few lifted eyebrows and some impolite stares as Lautrec, leaning heavily on his cane, tapped his way slowly toward his table in the rear. He did his best to ignore these new tourists, who, unlike the regulars, were unaccustomed to seeing the crippled artist of Montmartre mingling with the crowd.

Arriving at his private table, he sat down quickly and ordered a vermouth. The waitress nodded, knowing that this would be the first of many such orders from Monsieur Lautrec throughout the evening. Lautrec laid his cane aside and scanned the room quickly, his piercing, alert eyes taking in every person in the crowd, every customer at the bar, every dancer on the floor. The band played loudly, the drinks flowed, and the crowd watched, captivated by the dancers who swung their skirts and kicked their legs up higher and higher. The yellow lights overhead pierced through the cigarette smoke that hung in a filmy haze over their heads, giving the dance floor a dreamlike quality.

But Lautrec saw through the fantasy. He knew many of the dancers intimately and was acquainted with their personal struggles with illness, lost loves, poverty, and despair. He understood them as unique human beings who, through their craft, managed to earn a living distracting others from their own pain and from the tedium of daily life. But Lautrec the artist accepted this, as he had accepted his own disappointments. "One is ugly, but life is beautiful," he would often tell his friends.

Sipping his vermouth, he removed a sketch pad from his coat pocket, placed it on the table in front of him, and set immediately to work. The minutes passed quickly as Lautrec drew with feverish intensity, raising his eyes momentarily to study the crowd, then lowering them again to transfer his vision to paper. Unlike the Impressionist painters of preceding decades, Lautrec was a realist. He did not embellish what he saw, but rather sought to record things as they were. His goal was "to see and to put down," and he remained, throughout his life, a student of character. He found people, not landscapes, endlessly fascinating and concerned himself solely "with their burden of spirit and flesh and the stories of their minds," according to biographer Jean Bouret.

The minutes turned to hours, the dance hall filled, and the band played on. Lautrec filled another sketch pad, then another. He ordered a second drink, then a third, then a fourth. Amazingly, his hand never wavered—his concentration remained intense.

Few would have guessed, had they observed this small figure drawing furiously at his table, that they were in the presence of a count—a man who, at one time, stood to inherit one of the greatest fortunes in all of southern France. (At this point, Lautrec's status as heir was dubious, as his father disapproved of his lifestyle, and had supposedly threatened to disinherit him.) And here at the Moulin Rouge, in the midst of Paris's notorious nighttime entertainment establishments, Lautrec was far from his roots. He was the only surviving child of aristocratic parents— who were also first cousins—and therefore belonged to the highly privileged noble class.

But any hopes he once had of leading the leisurely life of a wealthy gentleman were put aside when, as a boy, he fractured both his legs and was diagnosed with a rare and incurable bone disease. As his mother tried to hide her guilt and his father his disappointment, young Henri turned to art as an outlet for his innate passion and intellect. Throughout his childhood, as the rest of his extended family enjoyed a life of fox hunting, athletics, and social events, Lautrec was frequently confined to his bed, with only his mother and his sketch pad to keep him company. (There are some who claim that Lautrec's artistic success was a direct result of his physical disability, but this explanation is overly simplistic and denies the inherent interest and talent he displayed at a very young age.)

Lautrec spent countless nights observing, sketching, and drinking at the Moulin Rouge nightclub, seen here with its spinning red windmill above the doorway. The artist was inspired to create many paintings and lithographs of the Moulin Rouge's performers and patrons.

In his Montmartre studio Lautrec paints At the Moulin Rouge: The Dance. *When it was finished, the painting was hung in the entrance of the nightclub.*

His family was only mildly surprised when, at age 18, Lautrec decided that he wanted to go to Paris to study art. With the help of his mother, his uncle Charles, and his art tutor René Princeteau, he got his wish. Between the years 1882 and 1887, he apprenticed under portrait painters Léon Bonnat and Fernand Cormon. At Cormon's studio he distinguished himself as a superb draftsman and was respected for his precise technique. After several years of studying and copying his teachers and their predecessors,

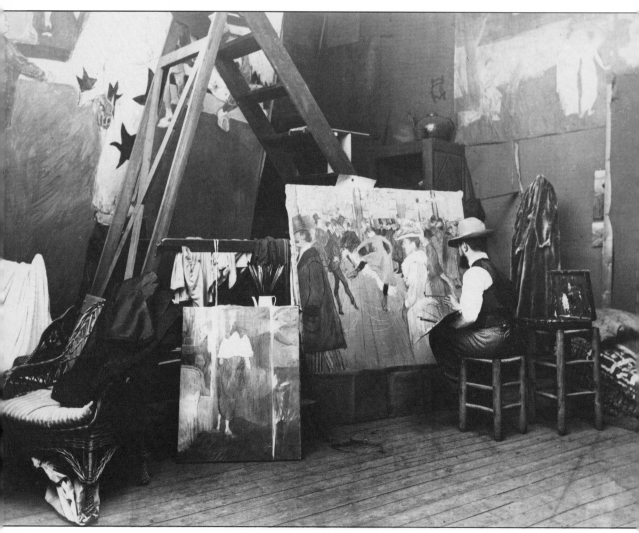

Lautrec began to develop his own style. Unlike the Impressionist painters, who used pastel tones, short brush strokes, blurred outlines, and layers of color, Lautrec preferred bold tones, long, sweeping brush strokes, defined outlines, and large areas of color. And though he was labeled a nonconformist by his colleagues, his work was well received at exhibitions in both France and Belgium.

After four years on his own, an opportunity presented itself that would greatly enhance Lautrec's artistic career. Joseph Oller and Charles Zidler, the owners of the Moulin Rouge nightclub, commissioned him to make a poster to advertise their establishment. Lautrec was flattered by their request and promised them a picture that would appeal to every Parisian.

Oller had already shown his admiration for Lautrec's work through previous purchases. *At the Cirque Fernando: The Ringmaster* was Lautrec's "first great pictorial experiment," in the opinion of 20th-century art critic Douglas Cooper, and his first painting of the circus (since boyhood he had remained an ardent fan of Le Cirque Fernando with its host of daring, athletic, and colorful performers). Lautrec had finished the painting in 1888 and Oller had purchased it the following year, hanging it in the foyer for the opening of the Moulin Rouge. The next year, Oller bought from Lautrec *At the Moulin Rouge: The Dance* and hung it in the nightclub's entrance as well. The picture shows two of the club's most popular performers— tall, debonair Valentin-le-Désossé (The Boneless) and daring, flashy, impetuous Louise Weber, known as La Goulue (The Glutton).

It was to these two individuals that Lautrec now turned for inspiration for the new poster. Night after night, hour after hour, he sketched the voluptuous red-haired dancer and her graceful partner as they entertained the crowds. When he felt he had made enough studies of his subjects, Lautrec set himself to the task of creating a perfect lithograph.

Unlike an oil painting that is produced on canvas or cardboard, a lithograph is a printed impression of an image that has been drawn directly on a specially prepared slab of stone or metal plate. The artist draws the image in reverse using a wax crayon or greasy ink, then dampens it with water and rolls it with ink. The outlined (greasy) areas accept the ink as the moist areas repel it. The image is then filled in, one color at a time, until complete. When paper is placed over the inked plate, the image is transferred (right side up) to it, and an original lithograph is produced. An advantage to this technique is that an unlimited number of prints of the same image can be made, making possible mass production of artwork.

Lautrec had been experimenting with lithography for more than five years with impressive results. He had long admired the work of the French caricaturist and painter Honoré Daumier (1808–79), who was considered "the father of lithography" and had produced more than 4,000 lithographs for various periodicals. Lautrec was also attracted to the clean lines and flattened images of Japanese woodcuts, which used a similar method. But to admire lithographs is one thing, and to reproduce them quite another. It requires that artists "master the technique and temperament of their plate and ink as tools" and execute their drawings with the skill and precision of a draftsman.

By 1891, when the owners of the Moulin Rouge commissioned Lautrec to do their poster, he had perfected this technique. He chose his subjects, made dozens of sketches, selected his colors, and went to work. In her 1973 book *Toulouse-Lautrec: His World,* biographer Sylvia Horwitz describes the final image:

> Lautrec's poster . . . was like an explosion. Center stage, but slightly off center: La Goulue, crackling like gunpowder. Her white petticoats are like foam boiling over, her pink blouse and yellow hair like exclamation points. She is framed by the angular gray silhouette of Valentin in the foreground, his left hand larger than life-size for effect. As

a backdrop for them both stands the audience—a taut, black human frieze relieved by the witty punctuation of ladies' collars and foolish hats.

The poster took several weeks to finish. Once complete, Lautrec wrote a letter to his mother that said: "I am still waiting for my poster to come out—there is some delay in printing. But it has been fun to do. I had a feeling of authority over the whole studio, a new feeling for me."

Lautrec was commissioned to design this poster for the owners of the Moulin Rouge in 1891. It caused tremendous commotion in the Paris art world and launched Lautrec's career as a commercial artist, helping to establish him as the founder of modern poster design.

When the poster was finally printed, it caused an un-
precedented commotion in the Paris art world. Nothing of
its kind had ever been seen before, and its release sparked
excessive commentary from club owners, fellow artists,
and writers. Francis Jourdain, a Paris journalist, wrote: "I
still remember the shock I had when I first saw the Moulin
Rouge poster. . . . This remarkable and highly original
[work] was, I remember, carried along the Avenue de
l'Opéra on a kind of small cart, and I was so enchanted that
I walked alongside it on the pavement."

Jean Adhémar, another writer of the day, observed:
"The flat tints, simple color-scheme and bold silhouettes,
and even Valentin's grimacing mask reveal the ardent
admirer of Japanese art; but the whole effect has an origi-
nality and force never seen before."

Like many of his contemporaries, Lautrec was fascinated by Japanese prints, which had first attracted the
attention of French artists in the early 1860s. The style
spread throughout the art world, but Lautrec adapted more
elements of Japanese art to his work than anyone else of
the time. From the Japanese he learned how to manipulate
contrasting curves and angles, along with flat areas of pure
color, to combine printed words and pictorial elements,
and to give unity to a composition.

Both Zidler and Oller were delighted with Lautrec's
work. The poster caused a sensation and brought hundreds
of new customers to their club.

After the success of the Moulin Rouge poster, many
other commissions followed, and Lautrec's career as a
commercial artist was launched. In the next 10 years, he
would produce 30 posters (in addition to his numerous oil
paintings and sketches), most of these portraying cabaret
singers, dancers, and theater personalities. In doing so he
fulfilled his desire to take fine art out of the realm of the
wealthy and elite and make it accessible to everyone.
Ironically, he also elevated certain aspects of ordinary
human behavior (getting dressed, lounging at a bar, wash-

ing clothes, and daydreaming) and made these the subjects of great art.

Lautrec, one of the best-loved chroniclers of the late 19th century, is also one of the most enigmatic and least understood personalities of his time. In the words of art critic Cooper, Lautrec "imposed a style on commercial art which is still unsurpassed. . . . His pictures are precious historic documents, which tell us as much as many a novelist or historian about the life and moral outlook of his generation. . . . He was one of the most engaging and amazing personalities in the history of art."

Henri, shown here at age three, was a precocious toddler and was nicknamed le petit bijou *(little jewel) by his grandmother.*

2

THE LITTLE GENTLEMAN

ON THE MORNING OF NOVEMBER 24, 1864, the rain came down in gusty sheets and pummeled the stained glass windows of the mansion high on the hill above the southern French town of Albi. As the dark clouds emptied their contents over the entire region of Languedoc, Count Alphonse de Toulouse-Lautrec paced nervously in the foyer of the Palais de Berbie, pausing every few minutes to listen for sounds from the upstairs bedroom.

But as the day wore on, the silence was broken only by occasional claps of thunder, and the darkness by intermittent flashes of lightning. The count, unaccustomed to having to wait for anything, tugged nervously at his thick beard and calmed himself with wine.

Finally, late in the day, the door to the bedroom opened and a nurse appeared. Countess Adèle had given birth to a fine healthy son, she told the count, and both mother and child were resting comfortably.

A few days later, when the weather had cleared, a glorious feast was held at the château to celebrate the birth of the couple's first child.

His parents had named him Henri after the count of Chambord, a descendant of Louis XV and the current pretender to the throne of France. Tiny, red-faced Henri Marie Raymond de Toulouse-Lautrec Monfa, swaddled in the finest embroidered blankets, remained blissfully unaware of the dozens of honored guests and townspeople who had come to express their congratulations. The count had spared no expense and the guests were treated to a sumptuous meal that included venison, pheasant, salmon, pâté de foie gras (goose liver), fresh cheeses, and fine wine.

The counts of Toulouse, of which Henri was now the youngest, could trace their heritage back to Charlemagne (ca. 742–814), king of the Franks, who first brought unity, civility, and education to the scattered tribes of medieval France and Germany, dominating all of central Europe by the end of his reign. Henri's family tree included men with reputations as consummate soldiers, passionate crusaders, loyal noblemen, and trustworthy administrators. For generations, the counts of Toulouse had remained the undisputed rulers of the region of Languedoc, having distanced themselves—both literally and figuratively—from the highly centralized politics of France. "The Counts of Toulouse had the prestige of great military leaders, and because they were cultivated lovers of the beautiful, they were able to enlarge their estates and even had hopes of uniting them into a kingdom," wrote biographer Jean Bouret in his 1962 book *The Life and Work of Toulouse-Lautrec*. "Quarrelsome and sensual, but also sensitive to a certain kind of nobility of character, and passionately attached to their native soil, the Toulouse-Lautrecs were aware of their strongholds, fields and vineyards as tangible realities and they stopped at nothing to keep them and acquire more."

In his marriage to Countess Adèle Tapié de Céleyran, Alphonse had further solidified the long-standing alliance between the house of Toulouse and that of another noble family, the Céleyrans. The two had often played together as children and had shown an early mutual affection.

The fact that they were first cousins was, rather than a deterrent to marriage, regarded quite favorably by both families. "The tendency to inter-marry persisted as it persists in most aristocratic families fearful of losing any part of long-cherished possessions by marriages outside the family and reluctant to taint their blood by mésalliances," explained biographers Lawrence and Elisabeth Hanson in their 1956 biography *The Tragic Life of Toulouse-Lautrec.* It is ironic that this union would make Henri "heir to some of the most princely holdings in the Midi [South of France]," and at the same time leave him with a legacy of almost unbearable emotional and physical pain.

As the firstborn son of Alphonse and the descendant of a thoroughly noble lineage, there were great expectations for young Henri right from the start. Like his father, he would fulfill his duty to the family by living the life of a gentleman. There would be no paid work for Henri, and it was assumed that he would spend his days in the saddle riding with the hounds and hunting for wild game, would dabble in the arts, and would eventually marry a woman from his own noble class, producing offspring to carry on the family name. No one attending the feast at the Lautrec mansion in Albi would have guessed any differently.

Soon after the festivities concluded, the couple hastened to the Château du Bosc, the principal estate of Henri's grandfather Raymond-Cassimir, known as the Black Prince. The château, an imposing medieval structure 30 miles north of Albi, was surrounded by vineyards, fields, and forests that served as hunting grounds for the residents. It was here, in the same house where his parents had once played together as children, that Henri would spend most of his childhood.

Upon their arrival, the couple received a joyful greeting from members of the extended family. The Black Prince himself was there to meet the carriage and was soon joined by Henri's grandmother, aunt, and two uncles. After each had expressed their congratulations and best wishes, they

Henri's father, Count Alphonse de Toulouse-Lautrec, would often venture away from the estate for long periods of time and was known to exhibit bizarre behavior, such as galloping through the woods dressed up in different costumes. Here he is shown in authentic Scottish garb.

toasted the birth with the finest spirits from the château's renowned wine cellar.

Later, the family sat down to a hearty meal in the formal dining room. Tired from the birth, the festivities, and the bumpy carriage ride from Albi, the couple excused themselves, put their new son to bed in a down-filled cradle, and retired to their chambers, anticipating their first restful night's sleep in several days.

In the coming months, young Henri grew accustomed to the rhythm of life at Le Bosc. Although the Toulouse-Lautrecs were thoroughly French, the influence of English aristocratic culture was apparent everywhere, from the tartan saddle blankets on the riding horses to the books on British history in the library. In a fashion similar to that of the inhabitants of the great country estates in Britain, the Lautrecs awoke to the sound of the hunting horn summoning the male members of the family, their guests, grooms, and whippers-in to the courtyard. As the women and children looked on from the windows, the men mounted their pure-blooded horses, gathered the hounds, and rode off into the morning mist for the day's hunting.

Countess Adèle Tapié de Céleyran was a doting mother to Henri, taking care of him personally rather than having the servants look after him.

Following this morning ritual, Henri and his mother commenced their own round of daily activities. Countess Adèle was a doting parent and though there were plenty of servants available, she preferred to look after Henri's needs herself. She bathed him in a fine porcelain tub, dressed him in velvet suits, and fed him cooked eggs, warm milk, and freshly baked bread. In her biography on Lautrec, Sylvia Horwitz observed: "Ensconced in this castle, Henri grew up to the touch of silk and velvet, the gleam of silver and fine porcelain, the clap of a hand and the stamp of a foot. It didn't take him long to discover his place [in society]."

In his first two years, Henri became a bright, curious, and talkative toddler who delighted his mother and the rest of his extended family with his precocious behavior. His grandmother nicknamed him *le petit bijou* (little jewel) and described him as "a real cricket . . . He sings from morning 'til night . . . [and] enlivens the whole household."

Adèle's brother married Alphonse's sister, and they had 14 children of their own. While further cementing the alliance between the two families, his numerous cousins provided Henri with an endless supply of playmates. The third floor of the château was the official playground for the youngest generation, and Henri quickly learned to fit in.

As he grew older, he led his cousins on raids to the pantry, drilled them in mock military maneuvers, and coerced their participation in countless practical jokes directed at the adults and their servants. "He was like quicksilver . . . never still," his mother remarked. In the warmer months, there was swimming in the nearby Tarn River, horseback riding, fishing, and games of croquet and soccer.

Like his father, Henri adored animals and life in the outdoors. He began taking riding lessons at age two and could soon sit on a horse as well as any of his older cousins. Alphonse was particularly proud. "Remember, my son," he wrote in a book on falconry that he gave to Henri, "that the only healthy life is the daylight life of the open air: whatever is deprived of liberty soon degenerates and dies. This little book . . . will teach you the value of outdoor life, and should you one day experience the bitterness of life, horses in particular, and also dogs and falcons, could be your treasured companions and help you to forget a little."

But despite his son's growing interest in the sporting life and his persistent questions about the daily hunts, Alphonse remained a somewhat distant parent. A confirmed eccentric, he was well known for his frequent displays of bizarre behavior. It was not unusual, for example, to see him galloping warriorlike through the woods, dressed in an authentic Turkish, Scottish, or Japanese costume, with a falcon perched on his arm. Townspeople had heard him singing love songs while washing his socks

René Princeteau made this drawing of Henri and his father, Count Alphonse, circa 1874. Princeteau, who was deaf, was an expert on the painting of horses and was Henri's first art teacher. He eventually moved to Le Bosc to further instruct his pupil.

in the rapids of the Tarn and had seen him brandishing a Japanese sword in a mock duel with an imagined foe.

The countess quietly tolerated her husband's penchant for cooking fresh game over the open fire of the salon and his long, often unexplained absences from the estate. (Upon his return, he would explain that he had been invited to a neighboring estate to hunt or had ordered his carriage to the horse races at Longchamps in Paris.) Despite her disapproval of his impulsive antics and self-centered lifestyle, she remained a faithful and supportive wife. Being surrounded almost constantly by relatives and family friends no doubt made it easier to tolerate her husband's emotional neglect. Had she lived in more isolated circumstances and without the pressure of family histories, she might have abandoned her weak marriage altogether. (Although they remained cordial to each other, their marriage lacked affection and mutual interests, lending support to the theory that convenience was one of the prime motivations for their union.)

When Henri was almost three years old, the countess gave birth to a second son. They named him Richard after King Richard the Lion-Hearted, whose wife was a Lautrec.

The child died in his first year, however, dashing Adèle's hopes that additional offspring would make Alphonse a more active participant in family life.

The weeks when the count managed to stay home were the times that young Henri liked best. He reveled in his father's companionship and wanted to go everywhere with him. Each day, he watched his father ride off to the hunt, his nose pressed against the window of his second-floor room. He waited until the last rider disappeared into the mist before turning to ask his mother the eternal question: "When will I be allowed to go?"

When the men returned from the day's hunting, the entire family sat down to a delicious meal, then retired to the salon for an evening of drawing, sculpting, handiwork, and storytelling. As the women knitted or sewed, the men re-created the images of the forest and the hunt from clay or sketched them in charcoal on dense, white paper.

It was during these quiet evening hours that Henri made his first drawings. Lying on his stomach on a warm sheepskin or fine Oriental rug, he watched his father and his uncle Charles as they sketched and drew. His uncle was particularly talented with the pencil, and Henri marveled at the ease with which he executed drawings of horses, hounds, and huntsmen. Henri did his best to imitate these and received praise and encouragement from Uncle Charles.

Night after night Henri would draw beside his uncle, lulled into quiet concentration by the warm, crackling fire, his father's humming, and the repeated tapping of his mother's knitting needles. He made the same drawings, mostly of horses, repeatedly and found that with practice the forms became clearer and more defined on the page. His mother praised his artwork, too, and observed that he had taken to it as easily as he had taken to horseback riding and swimming. She remembered that at his brother's christening, Henri had insisted on making his mark in the guest book. "You're too young to sign your name," she told him.

"Then I'll draw an ox," he replied, picking up the pen and detailing a bull-like creature in the margin.

By the age of four, Henri's precocious personality was well established. Much as his spirit thrived on the personal attention he received from his mother and older cousins, his intellect blossomed under Abbé Peyre, a Catholic priest whom the countess had chosen to be his academic tutor. Henri proved to be an excellent pupil, mastering his French letters at age three, and continuing with Latin, Greek, and English as he grew older.

His physical development, however, did not keep pace with his intellect. While his cousins grew steadily taller and stronger, Henri remained small and frail. His bright, gleaming eyes, tan skin, and healthy head of jet black hair contrasted sharply with his short, spindly legs and fragile bone structure. The Lautrec children formed a habit of marking their height on the wall of the third-floor corridor, and to Henri's great disappointment, his mark was always the lowest. Furthermore, the mark seemed to vary little from year to year. "Patience, mon petit bijou!" his grandmother told him.

But Henri was getting tired of waiting. Countess Adèle, equally frustrated and puzzled, ordered a groom to give Henri daily riding lessons to strengthen his legs. She took him on long walks around the estate, watched him swim in the river, and saw to it that he ate fresh, nutritious food. Despite her efforts, however, Henri remained a small and fragile boy.

When Henri was eight years old, he moved with his parents to Paris and began attending the Lycée Fontanes (now Lycée Condorcet), a private school for boys. The countess had decided that Henri needed a more comprehensive education than the good abbé could provide and was willing to leave Le Bosc so that he could have it. Biographers have speculated that she also hoped the move would encourage Alphonse to spend more time at home, thus providing Henri with a more accessible role model.

Henri's reaction to the decision is not known. Shortly after the move, however, he became very homesick, and for good reason: Paris in 1872 was "a beehive of activity." The Industrial Age was making its effects known in all corners of the world, and Paris was no exception. The capital of France was the center of high fashion, the arts, academics, and sports, and with its population of nearly 2 million, it was a city in constant motion. In many of the districts, living quarters were cramped and street noise was almost continuous. The sights and sounds on the bustling boulevards and hidden alleyways astounded young Henri, who was used to the quiet, pastoral setting of Le Bosc.

But it was not only the scenery that had changed—the people were different, too. The Parisians, Henri was quick to observe, were not at all like the quiet country folk of Albi. They were much more extroverted, given to spending long afternoons in crowded cafés where they thrived on intellectual conversation, emotional debate, and raucous, slapstick humor. Art critic John Russell, in his 1960 volume *Paris,* wrote: "Paris [has always been] a place where things happen on the street, rather than behind closed doors. . . . Parisians have a very low tolerance of boredom. . . . In their relations (or lack of relations) with one another, they are terrifyingly and everlastingly observant. Neutrality plays no part in Parisian life."

The fact that the Toulouse-Lautrecs hailed from a distant corner of the country did not prevent them from finding their niche in the city, however. As Russell also observed: "Anyone who can think on his feet and has some kind of reputation will be kindly received in Paris." This statement was as true in the 19th century as it is today, and explains the Lautrecs' relatively easy transition to city life. They took up residence in a house on the rue Faubourg St. Honoré, famous for its stately mansions and luxurious town houses. In this upper-class neighborhood, they asso-

Henri's mind seemed constantly to be on drawing. A page from his schoolbook shows sketches that he most likely made while he was supposed to be learning other school subjects. Today, this drawing is exhibited among others at the Toulouse-Lautrec Museum in Albi.

ciated with other aristocratic families and remained insulated from concerns of the bourgeoisie (middle class) and the poor.

The nearby Lycée Fontanes added a new dimension to Henri's academic life. He proved himself a competent student and, after his initial bout of homesickness, soon made several friends his own age. Two of these, Louis Pascal and Maurice Joyant, would form lifelong relationships with Henri, and Maurice would be instrumental in promoting his artistic career. Because of Henri's small stature and aristocratic heritage, the boys nicknamed him *le petit gentilhomme* (the little gentleman).

For two years, life went along rather smoothly. Henri's academic achievements placed him in the top 10 percent of his class even though he was its youngest member. His new life in no way diminished his interest in drawing, however, and his lesson books were filled with sketches of classmates, teachers, birds, horses, and dogs.

On weekends, Alphonse took him to the city's botanical gardens where together they observed and sketched. The count, an accomplished amateur artist himself, began taking Henri to visit his friend René Princeteau. Also somewhat of an eccentric, Princeteau was a respected animal painter who had been educated at the École des Beaux-Arts (official school of fine arts). He lived in an artists' colony located in a less-populated district at the farthest end of Faubourg St. Honoré. Though born deaf, Princeteau spoke adequately and was a well-respected teacher and artist.

It was at Princeteau's studio that Henri had his first real art lessons. Standing next to his father's easel, Henri experimented with line and color from his own small palette. His subjects did not vary from those he had sketched at Le Bosc, nor from those he scribbled in the margins of his schoolbooks. He sketched and painted what he knew.

Still, Princeteau was impressed. "From time to time Princeteau would stop his own work to look over the boy's sketches, praising a bird in flight, gravely correcting the leg muscles of a horse," wrote biographer Horwitz. "Henri glowed with pride."

Young Henri came to enjoy city life, making frequent trips to the racetrack with his father, to the theater with his mother, and to the circus with Princeteau. He delighted his friends Pascal and Joyant with his joking manner and good

This painting of Henri's father, Alphonse, mounted on a horse with a falcon perched on his hand, was completed by Henri in 1881, when he was just 16 years old.

humor, and on days off from school the three were nearly inseparable.

Henri's parents also found that Paris accommodated their lifestyle nearly as well as Albi. Alphonse still went riding every morning in the Bois de Boulogne (a grand park on the western edge of Paris) and took Henri to the public stables there for lessons. The count became a member of the Jockey Club, one of the last vestiges of the once powerful aristocracy left in Paris, and attended the horse races at Longchamps and Chantilly as often as possible. There are fewer recorded references pertaining to the activities of the countess during this time, but it is safe to assume that she spent much of her free time taking in the city's attractions, shopping, and attending theater and opera productions. As always, she remained a vigilant parent, putting Henri's needs before her own and watching over his progress with great care and concern.

Despite their overtly pleasant sojourn in the capital, a black cloud hung over this younger generation of Toulouse-Lautrecs. Henri's physical development remained far behind that of other boys his age, and he was especially weak in the legs. Toward the end of 1874, as he approached his 10th birthday, his absences from school became more frequent. He was often struck down by fevers, respiratory ailments, and trembling or weakness in his lower body. Paris doctors could find no explanation for this and advised his mother to take Henri back to the country. Perhaps there, they said, where the pace of life was slower, the sun warmer, and the mineral spas more plentiful, Henri might grow stronger.

Consequently, as biographer Jean Bouret explains: "Lautrec, too delicate for Paris, went back to Le Bosc and embarked on a round of spas, starting with Amélie-les-Bains which was recommended for decalcification and rickets."

Henri was glad to return to Le Bosc, where his homecoming was a joyous event for the rest of the extended family. Having maintained his precocity, he wasted no time in resuming leadership among his cousins. Bouret notes: "He had already begun to reveal his need for constant companionship, the need to feel that he was at the center of a group that protected him and over which he could exert his influence."

The weeks and months went by quickly as Henri filled them with swimming, riding, fishing, and lessons with his tutors. These activities were interrupted periodically for visits to Amélie-les-Bains, Lamalou-les-Bains, Barèges, and Nice. Countess Adèle took Henri faithfully to these health spas located throughout the southern regions of France hoping that the mineral content of their natural springs would restore strength to his ever weakening legs.

As Henri soaked himself for hours in the baths, which reportedly contained therapeutic amounts of arsenic and iron, his mother would sit patiently by and pray each time that he would be cured. Henri endured these prolonged soakings with characteristically good humor. He even managed to make friends with another frequent spa visitor named Etienne Devismes, a young boy who was also troubled by ill health. When not together at one of the spas, the two boys corresponded frequently, giving moral support when it was needed. The following excerpt from one of Henri's letters, written at Lamalou-les-Bains, illustrates the importance Henri placed on his friendship with Devismes: " 'Is he at Barèges?' That is the question I ask myself in the bath, in bed, and out walking. Indeed, all the ugliness of this hideous place vanishes . . . when I recall the hours you were so good to pass at my bedside. . . . I send you a hardy handshake."

But the spas, though pleasantly stimulating to the skin, did nothing to improve Henri's overall health. The effects of inbreeding were permanent, and despite his mother's fervent prayers, would soon result in tragedy for young Henri de Toulouse-Lautrec.

Henri drew this self-portrait in 1879. Because the artist had to remain in bed for long periods of time after he fractured his thigh bones, Henri had ample time to sketch to hone his drawing skills.

3

FATEFUL MISFORTUNES

SPRING WAS A GLORIOUS TIME in the Midi. The fields were filled with vibrant blossoms, the grapevines flowered on the hillsides, and the abundant forest came alive with the sounds of nesting birds and burrowing creatures.

Likewise, the inhabitants of Le Bosc greeted the new season with a flurry of activity. The house was swept, shutters opened, windows cleaned, and tapestries shaken out in the warm breezes. In the barn, grooms were kept busy with the arrival of newborn foals and with brushing out the rapidly shedding coats of the master's purebred hunters. A contagious restlessness pervaded the atmosphere both in and around the château. The promise of plentiful game and more daylight hours to hunt made the men fidgety and the animals skittish.

Henri sensed the animals' uneasiness and shared the men's eagerness for new adventures. From his bed on the second floor, he listened each morning for the whinny of his grandfather's horse Usurper as the groom led the animal across the courtyard. Through the doorway, he watched the servants bustling up and down the stairs and he called anxiously to his cousins as they ran by in the hall.

Always perceptive, Henri's senses had been sharpened by frequent confinements and prolonged inactivity. The spa visits had done nothing to improve the strength in his legs and he had hardly grown an inch in two years. The local doctors were baffled and could do nothing but recommend bed rest and restrict his physical activity. And so, while his cousins ran and played games on the lawn behind the château and galloped their ponies through the fields and jumped them over fences, Henri was limited to slow walks around the garden, leaning on his mother's arm for support.

On May 30, 1878, when Henri was 13 years old, the countess summoned yet another doctor to Le Bosc to examine her son. As Henri was pushing himself out of a chair, he slipped and fell on the polished wood floor. Crying out in pain, he grabbed his left leg, which was twisted at a sharp angle underneath him. The doctor confirmed a fracture of the thigh and immediately set the leg in a heavy plaster cast. Henri was taken once again to his bed and the leg was placed in traction.

He bore the setback with courage and good humor, for he believed, as all those around him did, that he would outgrow his illnesses and mature normally. Refusing to indulge in self-pity, he faced the future with optimism: "Don't cry over me," he wrote to one of his cousins shortly after the accident. "I'm not really worth it. . . . I receive lots of visitors and am terribly spoiled."

Drawing and sketching helped fill the long days and weeks of Henri's convalescence. His favorite subjects remained those he knew best: carriages, horses, and dogs. Producing their images on paper gave him great satisfaction and he enjoyed the vicarious feeling of movement he experienced through their creation. He was critical of his work, however, and would sketch the leg of a horse or the face of a dog repeatedly, for hours, until he felt he had it right.

When the fracture was sufficiently healed, Henri's mother whisked him off on yet another round of visits to the spas, with the hope of curing him. This, too, he tolerated with characteristic cheerfulness, choosing to turn the boring ritual of soaking into an opportunity to enlarge his repertoire of artistic subjects. "I am sending you the first watercolors I have done since my recovery," Henri wrote to his friend Charles Castelbon. "My menu isn't very varied, I've only [boats] and sailors to choose from. . . . My trees are like spinach. The Mediterranean is a devil to paint, precisely because it is so beautiful."

Encouraged by his steadfast interest in art, his mother kept him well supplied with charcoal, colored pencils, paper, and paints. "If drawing had been a pastime before, it now became a passion," wrote biographer Horwitz. "At his mother's insistence he continued studying with his tutors, but every moment stolen from Latin went to art. He tried his hand at portraits, oils, and pastels, becoming more and more self-critical. As his eye sharpened, so did his standards."

Henri had inherited the intensity of character and passion of feeling that was the hallmark of the Toulouse-Lautrecs, but because of his physical weakness it had remained somewhat suppressed. Now, however, these traits began to surface in his art. Drawing and painting became a much needed outlet for Henri's maturing physical and emotional energies and he approached them each day with a sense of purpose.

By the end of the year, Henri could walk about the grounds with assistance, his leg having mended completely but much more slowly than expected. Leaning on his wooden crutch for support, he accompanied Uncle Charles to a nearby field where the local militia was conducting drills. Artillerymen, dragoons, and officers soon filled his sketchbooks and were a distinct improvement over the caricatures he had scribbled in the margins of his Paris schoolbooks. These drawings, which today hang in the Toulouse-Lautrec Museum in Albi, are evidence of Henri's growing interest in the unique habits and personalities of individuals: a drill sergeant stands tall and unsmiling, arms crossed at the chest, feet wide apart; an enlisted man rests beside a tree, idly scratching his ear; and a young recruit, eager to please his superiors, earnestly practices handling his weapon.

It is significant to note that although Henri was constantly surrounded by some of the most beautiful and inspiring landscape in all of France, he seldom made it the focus of his work. Even at this early stage of his artistic development, he found physical movement and aspects of individual character (man or beast) much more intriguing. "Nothing exists but the figure," he later told his friend and biographer Maurice Joyant. "Landscape is nothing and should be nothing but an accessory. Landscape should be used only to make the character of the figure more intelligible."

Fifteen months after he fell from his chair, Henri met with yet another misfortune that his father described in a letter to a friend: "The second fracture was caused by a fall scarcely heavier than the first while he was out walking with his mother; he fell into a dried-up bed of a gulley no more than a few feet deep. While his mother went to get a doctor, Henri, far from bemoaning his misfortune, sat with his hands rigidly supporting his injured thigh."

The chance of two such accidents occurring so easily to a normal, healthy boy were slim. The attending doctors concluded, therefore, that Henri was the victim of a rare and incurable bone disease, which was the direct consequence of his parents' inbreeding. "It seems certain that Lautrec was suffering from polyepiphyseal dystrophy, or an underdevelopment of certain osseous (bone) tissues

Henri's uncle Charles was an avid supporter of his nephew's art. Himself an amateur artist, Charles encouraged Henri and gave him his first drawing lessons. Henri drew this portrait, Count Charles de Toulouse-Lautrec, *in 1882.*

that left his bones abnormally brittle," wrote biographers Philippe Huisman and M. G. Dortu in their 1973 book, *Toulouse-Lautrec.* "The result was that Henri . . . stopped growing. . . . At thirteen he was four feet eleven inches tall; as an adult he was still just about five feet tall—that is, not a dwarf, as he has sometimes wrongly been depicted, but a conspicuously short man. Moreover, while his head and torso were of normal adult size, his legs remained weak and stiff and abnormally stunted. It was this disproportion that gave his figure its curious aspect."

The second fracture, this time of the right leg, required another cast, more traction, and an equally long convalescence. On the surface, Henri maintained his usual optimism, but underneath his cheerful facade the effects of his isolation and despair were deeply felt. "I am alone most of the day," he wrote in his personal journal, *Zig Zag*. "I read for hours, my head aches. I draw and I paint as much as I can, until my hand gets tired—and when evening comes I wait to see whether [my cousin] Jeanne will come to visit me. She comes sometimes and I listen to her. She is so tall and beautiful, and I, I am neither tall nor beautiful."

As this journal entry indicates, Henri was indeed painfully aware of his physical difference and the fact that it made him less attractive to others, especially those of the opposite sex. Nevertheless, throughout his life, his passion for relationships in the form of friendship and romantic love remained as great as his passion for art. It is this paradox—the coexistence of a sensitive and ardent personality in a malformed body—that would be responsible for his greatest joys and his deepest despair.

In the two years following his second accident in August 1879, Henri endured "a monotonous existence," consisting mostly of frequent trips to the spas at Nice and Barèges (the countess still hoped they might do some good) and long confinements in the Château du Bosc. When he was 16 years old, Henri once again met his friend Etienne Devismes at the spas. Etienne was as devoted to writing as Henri was to sketching, and it was not long before they decided to collaborate on a book. "Cocotte" was the story of an old cavalry horse who responded to the sound of the bugle long after she was retired and put to more practical use. Henri was touched by the tale and set to work immediately on the illustrations. He produced 23 sketches in a remarkably short time and sent them to his friend with the following note: "I've done my best. If you want more, I'm your man."

The discipline required to complete this small but personally significant project had a positive effect on Henri and whetted his appetite for new artistic challenges.

Uncle Charles remained a strong advocate of his nephew's art and convinced the count that Henri should continue his formal instruction with Princeteau. The count, who no doubt struggled with a sense of guilt for precipitating his son's misfortune, as well as his own disappointment for having produced an imperfect heir, reluctantly agreed. Princeteau was then summoned to Le Bosc and became a long-term guest of the household.

At the same time that Henri was pursuing his art, he was presumed to be preparing for his baccalaureate exam. The test was administered by the French government and was taken by students of Henri's age as a prerequisite for higher education. But Henri's passion for art did not extend to Latin, Greek, mathematics, and other required subjects, and though he tolerated sessions of academic tutoring, he preferred to spend all of his free time painting and sketching.

In July 1881, Henri went to Paris to take the exam and failed. His reaction was typically lighthearted, and upon hearing the news, he ordered new calling cards from the printer with the inscription: Henri de Toulouse-Lautrec: Exam Flunker.

His pride would not allow him to appear unintelligent, however, and he spent the next several months preparing in earnest for the second attempt. In November of that year he took the exam in Toulouse and passed. The experience left him relieved but most unimpressed with the educational system and its administrators: "At last the jury at Toulouse pronounced me acceptable, in spite of the nonsense I dished out to them!! I quoted passages from Lucain, who doesn't exist, and the professor, wanting to appear erudite, received me with open arms," he wrote to his friend Etienne.

The year 1881 proved significant for another reason, too, for it was during his 17th year that Henri completed his first true portraits. He began with his most accessible subject—his mother—painting her in shades of yellow and brown with some red and green highlights, seated at a small table, drinking a cup of tea. The painting was conceived in the Impressionist style, with which Princeteau had Henri experiment. It is characterized by varied, short brush strokes and places great importance on light and colors (as represented by the works of the Impressionist painters Édouard Manet, Edgar Degas, and Claude

One of the first portraits Henri painted was this one of his mother having breakfast in the Château de Malromé. Feeling partly responsible for her son's health condition and his inability to pursue sport, Countess Adèle constantly commended Henri's artwork and urged him to continue painting.

Monet), the portrait was executed with significant skill and, according to Lawrence and Elisabeth Hanson, represented "quite an astonishing advance" for Henri. The countess praised the work and encouraged him to do more. Henri's second portrait was of his cousin Raymond and a young rooster. In this work the artist's ability to capture individual mannerisms manifested itself more clearly. Henri managed to convey the young aristocrat's strident personality in caricaturelike style, while showing a distinctly defiant attitude on the part of the bird.

For his third portrait subject, Henri chose a local drunkard, Père Mathias. There were two reasons for this. First, the old man was easily accessible (he was nearly always at the local tavern) and could be counted on to sit still at his table for hours at a time. Second, Henri was discovering his affinity for portraying individuals and for representing various aspects of human nature through his paintings. "He was fascinated by inebriety," wrote Lawrence and Elisabeth Hanson. "The choice of subject was strange in a boy of that age—strange and significant—but his treatment of it . . . was even more so; he painted with the directness of vision that was to be one of his outstanding contributions to painting—without sentimentality, without exaggeration, without pity too, as if he were some lynx-eyed immortal immune to all human feelings except that of curiosity."

Together, these three portraits mark the beginning of Henri's serious commitment to art. He continued to study under Princeteau, but it soon became clear that he needed more than the kind instructor could offer him. With the help of Uncle Charles, Henri convinced his parents that he must return to Paris and seek more formal training.

In March 1882, Henri and his mother left for the capital, arriving a few days later at their residence on the rue Faubourg St. Honoré. This time, there was little reason for homesickness. Le Bosc offered nothing but old memories and the constant reminder of the active life in which he could never fully participate. Paris, on the other hand, was full of promise. A glittering, fast-moving city full of artists, intellectuals, and innovators, it was a proving ground where Henri's ambitions and developing talents might be valued and his physical limitations could be overlooked.

Through a friend in Albi, the countess had obtained a letter introducing her son to the eminent artist and instructor Léon Bonnat. Bonnat, whose reputation was well known throughout the city, was one of the most famous portrait painters of his day. As biographer Hanson wrote: "Léon Bonnat was then in his fiftieth year, a ramrod of a man externally and internally, much pleased with himself . . . commissioned again and again by the government which loaded him with honors, and reputed the most difficult artist to persuade to undertake a commission."

Bonnat admitted Henri to his studio somewhat reluctantly, for he had already established his own small group of apprentices over whom he presided in the strictest manner. He reveled in his authority over his pupils but did not, in the fashion of a true master, desire the success of any of his followers, preferring to reserve the arena of achievement for himself. His painting style, though highly regarded in his time, was nonetheless extremely conservative, completely void of innovation or variation in technique, and copying precisely the techniques of the old masters of the Romantic period, who included Jacques-Louis David, Jean-Auguste-Dominique Ingres, and Eugène Delacroix.

As might be expected, Henri found his own style, which had already developed several noticeable and consistent characteristics, wholly at odds with that of his instructor. He did his best to conform, however, because he respected Bonnat's position and experience. Bonnat, on the other hand, had little regard for Henri's work. "You may be wondering what kind of encouragement I am getting from Bonnat," Henri wrote to Uncle Charles in May 1882. "He tells me 'Your painting isn't bad . . . but your drawing is quite frankly atrocious.' So I must pluck up courage and start again, when I've rubbed out all my drawings with breadcrumbs."

Henri's apprenticeship at the atelier (studio) lasted little more than a year. In 1883, Bonnat closed his studio in Montmartre, a section of Paris located on a hill that was known for attracting bohemian artists. He had been appointed professor at the École des Beaux-Arts, the premier school of fine arts in France and one of the greatest institutions of its kind in the world. This event, which at first seemed to be another setback for Henri, would in time prove to be a stroke of good luck.

In the weeks following the closing of Bonnat's studio, Henri was at a loss for what to do next. But his will to pursue his artistic studies prevailed, and he soon summoned the courage to find a way to continue. Joined by several other students from Bonnat's studio, he approached another successful painter, Fernand Cormon. They were ecstatic when Cormon offered to take them on as pupils and agreed to allow his studio in Montmartre to serve as their hub of inspiration. For Henri, the change came just at the right moment.

This photograph of Fernand Cormon's studio was taken around 1885. Lautrec (wearing a hat, seated at the far left) unfortunately discovered that Cormon (seated at easel) was a less demanding teacher than Léon Bonnat was. Nevertheless, Lautrec remained a student of Cormon's for five years, during which he polished his technique and gained confidence in his work.

4

THE MAKING OF
AN ARTIST

FERNAND CORMON WAS A RENOWNED PAINTER who was held in high regard by the artistic community in Paris. He attracted aspiring artists from all parts of France and as far away as the United States and Australia. In these ways he was very much like Léon Bonnat. It is here, however, that the similarities between the two men ended. Whereas Bonnat was demanding, strict, and quick to censor nontraditional work, Cormon was cheerful, lenient, and tolerant of new ideas.

Early in 1883, Cormon welcomed Monsieur Lautrec (as 18-year-old Henri was now addressed) and other refugees from Bonnat's studio with open arms. Lautrec, who was already developing the discipline he would later need as a professional artist, was delighted to return to work. Each morning at half past eight o'clock, he left his mother's house and rode the carriage to 10, rue Constance, Montmartre. After the driver helped him down from the seat, Lautrec leaned heavily on his wooden cane and slowly made his way to the studio door and into the workroom where the other students were setting up their easels. The pupils, who came from diverse economic and geographic backgrounds, included three of Lautrec's friends from the Midi: René Grenier, François Gauzi, and Henri Rachou. Tristan and Émile Bernard, Adolphe Albert, Vincent van Gogh, and Charles Lucas were among the others who had come to Cormon for instruction and were now in various stages of their formal training. The group's self-proclaimed leader, however, was Louis Anquetin, known as "the giant from Normandy." He was "three years older and sixteen inches taller than Lautrec, with rough-cast Nordic features, an iron constitution, muscles like whipcord, and an extraordinary gift for drawing and for horsemanship," wrote biographer Jean Bouret. "Anquetin appointed himself Lautrec's protector, sheltering him from horseplay and practical jokes and, most important of all, giving him confidence in his talent."

Practical jokes aside, the atmosphere of Cormon's studio was one of camaraderie and friendly competition. As the 30 students worked diligently to copy the model posed in front of them, they often discussed the merits and shortcomings of various styles of painting. Cormon himself adhered to a traditional and strictly academic style, which involved painting subjects that conformed to the traditions of the day. These were based on the teachings at the École des Beaux-Arts, and included landscapes, portraits, and nudes. However, he encouraged—much to his credit—discussion and experimentation with other styles, including that of the controversial Impressionists. "It is doubtful whether [Lautrec] saw an Impressionist canvas before 1882," wrote biographers Elisabeth and Lawrence Hanson. (It is likely, however, that his former art tutor, René Princeteau, had seen Impressionist work and had encouraged Lautrec to experiment with this technique.) "At Cormon's . . . the names of Manet, Monet,

Renoir, Degas—to say but four—were quoted as the heroes or the villains of the day according to the point of view of the speaker, and their work [was] discussed interminably."

Much later, both Anquetin and Émile Bernard would rebel against Cormon's conservative painting style. They were subsequently expelled from the studio for their unwillingness to practice several basic techniques that Cormon felt were a necessary part of every painter's training. Despite his personal exuberance and developing independence, Lautrec submitted willingly to the traditional and often tedious exercises put forth by his teacher. He painted Cormon's subjects, which were taken from Greek myths and tales of ancient civilizations, without protest. Images of nymphs, goddesses in flowing robes, Trojan warriors, and aged monarchs filled his canvases during his first year as an apprentice. "I am here to learn my job," he told his friend Gauzi, "but not to let my individuality be absorbed." At the tender age of 18, Lautrec seemed to understand that he could successfully develop his own style only after he had first learned and practiced—over and over again—the most basic principles of drawing and painting.

Twice each week, Lautrec and the others presented their work for Cormon's criticism. As he made the rounds of the studio, the teacher paused at each easel to observe the students' progress and technique. Possessing a dramatic flair, Cormon dispensed his comments and criticisms quickly and honestly. His reputation for fairness endeared him to the majority of the students, but Lautrec had mixed feelings about the master's leniency. "Cormon's comments are far milder than those of Bonnat," he wrote in a letter to his uncle Charles dated February 18, 1883. "Whatever you show him he warmly approves. It will surprise you, but I like his reaction less. Indeed, the lashes of my old master put ginger into me and I didn't spare myself. Here, on the other hand, I feel a little diffident, and have

This 1883 allegory, The Spring of Life, *by Lautrec is an example of the type of work that the aspiring artists at Cormon's atelier were taught. Lautrec and several other apprentices eventually abandoned this academic method and developed their own individual styles.*

to make an effort conscientiously to produce a drawing which will impress Cormon no differently from many another."

In conversation, the students referred to Cormon as Père La Rotule (Father Swivel Joint) because he was tall, lanky, and double-jointed. With the exception of Anquetin and Bernard, the apprentices thrived under his tutelage and the "atmosphere of uninhibited bohemianism" that characterized the atelier. But the unconventional lifestyle with which Lautrec would later be associated was quite unsettling to him at first. In a letter to his grandmother he wrote, "I am against my will leading a truly Bohemian life and finding it difficult to accustom myself to this milieu. I am particularly ill at ease on the Butte Montmartre in that I feel myself constrained by a whole heap of sentimental considerations which I simply must put out of my mind if I am to achieve anything."

During the five years that Lautrec apprenticed at Cormon's studio, La Butte (the hill), as Montmartre was affectionately called, was undergoing rapid change. Biographer Bouret described Montmartre in its early days as "a village among market-gardens and flour-mills, a favorite goal of lovers on their Sunday outing, a hiding place for unmarried mothers and wild boys, a lucky dip for professional foster mothers and the Waifs and Strays Society, and a refuge for lovers of silence and the rustic scene." As Paris's population expanded and the effects of the industrial revolution made both travel and leisure more accessible, the hill was "colonized from the base upwards," becoming a settlement for artists, entertainers, prostitutes, and working-class citizens. But despite its increasing number of inhabitants, Montmartre "still asserted its independence by fostering a slightly individual atmosphere, a psychology tinged with anarchy."

Like any young person standing on the threshold of adulthood, Lautrec was torn between his familiar, comfortable past and his new, promising, and uncharted future. The values and habits he had formed while living the aristocratic, conservative lifestyle of his childhood came into increasing conflict with the influence of his peers and the liberal, pleasure-seeking culture of Montmartre. It seemed inevitable that the experimental and somewhat rebellious attitude of the Montmartre culture would seep into Lautrec's life and work.

Very gradually, and only after he had painstakingly mastered the basic techniques of his trade, did Lautrec begin to move away from tradition on both fronts. He continued to reside with his mother in their house on the rue Faubourg St. Honoré, but he began spending more and more of his free time carousing and cavorting with his artist friends. After the day's work at Cormon's studio, they would adjourn to one of the local cafés or to Grenier's home for an afternoon of wine guzzling and playacting. Like his father, Lautrec loved to dress up in outlandish costumes and was delighted to find that several of his colleagues also enjoyed this diversion. Photographs from this period show Lautrec, Grenier, Gauzi, and their friend Métivet dressed as women, Japanese soldiers, American Indians, and Scottish Highlanders.

Within the circle of young and aspiring artists, Lautrec found both companionship and authentic support for his work. After his first year at Cormon's atelier he relaxed

Lautrec drinks wine with friends in the garden of the Moulin de la Galette, a café-restaurant with a large dance area. He used the café as the subject of many of his works, including his first large-scale painting of a dance scene.

visibly and developed many close friendships. "I never saw him make a mistake in his judgement of our comrades, for he was a skilled psychologist," wrote fellow art student Henri Rachou. "He opened up his heart only to those whose friendship he had tested. At times he treated others with a casualness akin to cruelty. But he had perfect manners if he felt like it, and he showed an exact sense of the correct attitude to adopt in all circumstances. I have never seen in him either effusiveness or [excessive] ambition. He was first and foremost an artist." François Gauzi wrote: "Lautrec had the gift of endearing people to him, all his friends were devoted to him, he never addressed a provocative word to anyone and never sought to exercise his wit at the expense of others; with the aid of his brush he poked fun at his fellow creatures and himself alike."

Lautrec used his superbly developed sense of humor to his advantage in countless situations. Quite often, he used it as a distraction from his physical appearance, which, though he had ostensibly accepted it, still pained him on a deeper level. His mother knew, as almost no one else could, the extent of her son's distress. "Countess Adèle was not deceived when Henri jokingly referred to himself as 'half-pint' and drew ridiculous caricatures of a dwarfish painter to make her laugh. Though they never spoke openly about it, she was acutely aware of her son's suffering," wrote Sylvia Horwitz.

Rachou, Grenier, Gauzi, Anquetin, and the other apprentices included Lautrec in all of their discussions and activities. Nevertheless, when the conversation turned to matters of romance, women, and sexual conquests, Lautrec remained uncharacteristically silent. Having no real experience in these areas, he could not participate in their friendly joking or add to their romantic tales. In Lautrec's time, society was less understanding and accepting of physical differences than today. Although he easily secured lifelong friendships and eventually won the respect of his professional community, love relationships posed an altogether different challenge. Gradually, he came to realize that his disability would make it difficult, if not impossible, to win the love of a woman of his class and to settle down to a "normal" family life.

And so, whenever the subject of romance was openly discussed at Cormon's studio, Lautrec began to match his colleagues' tales with his own manufactured stories. Horwitz wrote, "His grasp for Parisian slang was as colorful as anybody's. . . . He could even try and top the others by announcing that he personally would settle only for a strong woman who had a lover uglier than he was. But it was all a sham and a cover-up, and he knew it."

In a gesture of both sympathy and friendship, the apprentice Charles Lucas introduced Lautrec to Marie Charlet. Marie was a prostitute with a tragic past and a history of survival on the streets. She accepted Lautrec as an equal—as a man with human feelings and human needs. For a while, this was enough for Lautrec and he found their casual relationship highly satisfying. According to Bouret, Marie seemed equally content with the arrangement and even "brought to him, with no sign of jealousy, such of her girl-friends as were in need of affection."

But their relationship was short-lived. Marie grew tired of Lautrec (whom she referred to as her "darling coathanger") and left him abruptly with no explanation. The sensitive Lautrec, though inwardly distraught, weathered the crisis by plunging deeper into his work and drinking more wine. He continued to seek the affection of other working girls, however, a habit that would continue throughout the rest of his life. "With the instincts of a wounded animal, Lautrec sought the protection of darkness and secrecy," wrote Horwitz. "He looked for affection among those as scarred as himself. . . . None of them knew how to hold a teacup properly, but each treated him like any other man. Victims of fate, as he was, they lived and let live in a world where nothing human caused surprise."

Lautrec moved into Lily and René Grenier's Montmartre apartment in 1884. The three companions, shown here with another friend, would often entertain artists from Cormon's studio at their flat.

Lautrec's coming-of-age had a liberating effect on his art as well. For several years, he had remained faithful to Cormon's thorough yet stylistically limited academic teaching and was now moving more confidently into his own style. He continued to abhor landscapes and ignored most of the technical innovations put forth by the Impressionists. Of those Impressionists who were actively painting in the mid to late 1880s, including Camille Pissarro, Pierre-Auguste Renoir, Paul Cézanne, Berthe Morisot, Edgar Degas, and Alfred Sisley, only Degas influenced Lautrec to any great degree.

In 1883, Countess Adèle purchased a 125-acre estate, Château de Malromé, near Bordeaux, which she used from then on as her main residence. Lautrec spent the summer there with her but returned to Paris alone in the fall. He moved in with René and Lily Grenier in their apartment at 19, rue Fontaine, Montmartre, the following year. The apartment had become the meeting place for many of the young artists from Cormon's studio, and Lily—a pretty, freckled redhead—was a willing hostess. A former model for Degas, she was described by Gauzi as "very desirable and constantly surrounded by a group of admirers." Lautrec's respect for René's friendship prevented him from making romantic advances toward Lily, however, and their relationship remained platonic. "The comradeship between them never faltered," wrote Gauzi.

It was Lily Grenier who, late in 1885, introduced Lautrec to her former boss, Edgar Degas. Lautrec was immediately taken by the man, 30 years his senior, whose studio was located directly across the street from the Greniers' apartment. Lautrec had long admired Degas's work, which he felt had more depth and meaning than that of the other Impressionists. Lautrec had much in common with Degas, including a love of horses, circus performers, and dancers. They also shared a profound dislike for landscapes and a deep interest in the psychology of individuals.

Their artistic philosophies and techniques were also closely aligned. Both were superb draftsmen who approached their subjects realistically and with extreme objectivity. Both concerned themselves with movement and athleticism (Degas with racehorses and ballerinas, Lautrec later with cabaret performers, acrobats, and showgirls) and delighted in portraying the individual in the context of his or her work. Lastly, they shared an aristocratic attitude that was often perceived as misanthropy (a harshly critical view of mankind). "[Degas] was a man who gave the impression of having been everywhere and known everyone worth knowing (one gathered that these were few) and to have formed decided opinions on all," wrote Lawrence and Elisabeth Hanson. "But Degas had his kindly side, when he did not deal with the pretentious but the humble, which Toulouse-Lautrec found admirable."

Although Lautrec was greatly influenced by Degas's work, he was from a newer, highly experimental, and more progressive generation than the old master. A combination of his innate talent and intelligence as well as the prevailing social trends of his time would compel Lautrec to form his own original style. During his last year at Cormon's studio, he developed a reputation as a nonconformist. His friend Gauzi observed, "Lautrec [now] shows disdain for the subject matter recommended by Cormon. . . . He considers that the Greeks ought to be left to the Pantheon [from the Greek, meaning "a shrine to the gods"; the Roman emperor Hadrian had the Pantheon built in Rome ca. A.D. 120–27] and firemen's helmets to David [whose *Oath of Horatii* (1784) shows three Roman soldiers in classical helmets preparing for war]. He derides painters who [are] obsessed by the technicalities of their profession."

At the age of 21, Lautrec was maturing both as an individual and as an artist. At Cormon's atelier, he had gained the confidence he needed to be an innovator, a painter who would influence those who would follow him for decades to come. Finally, he felt ready to test himself— and his art—in the world outside the studio door.

Lautrec found the model for The Laundress *(1888) on the street—she was a working-class girl who delivered laundry to clients in order to earn money. Lautrec treated all of his subjects the same: in his eyes a portrait of a prostitute and one of a princess were of equal stature.*

5

THE WORLD OUTSIDE

MORE AND MORE, Lautrec found himself drawn into the bohemian lifestyle of Montmartre. He began keeping "artists' hours," which meant long days of portrait painting and sketching (he used a friend's garden as a temporary studio, storing his supplies in a small wooden shed) followed by nights of socializing, discussion, and carousing at one of the many cabarets that were springing up in the district. The most auspicious of these was Le Chat Noir (The Black Cat), opened in 1881 by Rodolphe Salis. A former cartoonist, Salis had become a successful businessman when he converted a former post office into an enticing *cabaret-chantant* (music hall) and recruited some of the most promising entertainers in Paris to perform there.

Lautrec's initial reaction to Le Chat Noir was less than enthusiastic, but his curiosity would not allow him to stay away for more than a few nights. A student of character, he was as intrigued by the customers as he was by the performers themselves. "The cream of Paris society crowded into these cramped quarters to drink bad beer and enjoy rubbing shoulders with the rabble and watching women of easy virtue pick up customers, while [the singers] reeled off . . . songs amid the smoke of half-Havanas [cigars]," wrote Jean Bouret.

Seated at a table by himself or with a group of his artist friends, Lautrec sketched the performers, prostitutes, and customers with the same dedication as he had the models at Cormon's studio. His hand was more sure now and his artistic confidence higher than it had ever been before. He felt at home in the smoke-filled room where singers performed night after night before raucous crowds. Young and old, rich or poor, they came to Le Chat Noir to drown their troubles in alcohol and song, or at least to find a temporary distraction from the tedium of everyday life.

In this decade of expansion and industrialization, however, nothing in Montmartre remained the same for long. In 1885, Salis sold Le Chat Noir to Aristide Bruant and the club was henceforth known as Le Mirliton [from *vers de mirliton,* meaning trashy verse, for which Bruant was famous]. The new owner was an imposing character—a tall, husky man with a booming voice and a caustic wit. Born into poverty, he had learned to survive by singing songs and reciting verses in the Paris cafés and music halls. He possessed a poet's ear for lyrical verse and later composed his own songs. Gradually, Bruant saved enough money to purchase his own club, and when he did, he threw himself into the project with tremendous enthusiasm. He posted a sign out front that read: RENDEZVOUS FOR THOSE SEEKING TO BE ABUSED. Customers approaching Le Mirliton after dark soon discovered that Bruant meant what he said. Standing just outside the entrance, he greeted his customers with epithets such as "scoundrel," "pig," "tart," "imbecile," "cutthroat," and "pimp." Once inside, however, those who endured the verbal lashing at the entrance were treated to a night of entertainment unmatched by any cabaret in Paris.

Lautrec liked Bruant immediately, shared his realism, and found his earthy sense of humor refreshing. As their friendship grew, Bruant commissioned Lautrec to illustrate his songsheets and to contribute sketches for his new magazine, *Le Mirliton*. Lautrec became a nightly patron and Bruant would announce his arrival with characteristic humor: "Silence gentlemen . . . here comes the great painter Toulouse-Lautrec with one of his friends and a punk I don't know!" Lautrec was then treated to free drinks while he sketched the performers. Several hours of sketching, drinking, and verbal jousting with Bruant would have been quite enough for most people—but not for Lautrec. Shortly after midnight, he would leave the waitress a generous tip, bid farewell to his host, and make his way slowly to the door. He would then hail a horse-drawn taxi and continue the evening at one of the other familiar cabarets, two dozen of which were already scattered throughout the city.

Although Lautrec's affinity for nighttime entertainment provided him with endless portrait and sketching subjects, it also provided reinforcement for his already pronounced drinking habit. He told his friends that he drank "only a little but often," and was equally content with a bottle of beer or wine as he was with a glass of brandy. The reasons for Lautrec's drinking have been endlessly speculated upon, but there is no clear consensus among either biographers or historians as to its actual cause. From his letters to his family, it is clear that he did experience some physical pain and fatigue in his legs that increased with age. In the beginning, alcohol may simply have been a convenient and effective analgesic.

But there were nonphysical reasons for the habit as well. The psychological isolation Lautrec endured because of his disability was almost certainly compounded by the fact that he was an innovative artist. The latter part of the 19th century, unlike earlier decades, was a time when those who earned a living in the arts were increasingly ostracized from mainstream society. With the advent of the Industrial Age, there was a philosophical shift in the value of creativity that led to an emphasis on product over process. People wanted things to be both easier and faster than ever before. As art historian Sam Hunter observes, this shift had a negative effect on artists of the Post-Impressionist era:

> The Impressionists belonged to a healthy social organism; they could still find a common ground in society as well as among themselves. The Post-Impressionists lived in a different moral atmosphere. They could not put their trust in common life, and they formed no real community among themselves. . . . The careers of [Post-Impressionists] Gauguin, Van Gogh and Lautrec represent a heroic effort to find their places in a world which did a minimum to make the progressive artist welcome.

Whether Lautrec's drinking was caused more by internal factors than by external ones—physical more than emotional—is still a subject for debate. Whatever the reason, it became a firmly entrenched habit by the time he had reached his late twenties. The fact that his artistic production remained prodigious is nothing short of miraculous. Lautrec was determined to live intensely, and he soon discovered that rather than dull his perceptions, alcohol had the effect of sharpening them. At his private table at Le Mirliton, Lautrec sipped brandy, wine, or vermouth from one hand and sketched diligently with the other. "He lived through his eyes," wrote Jean Bouret. "He believed only in what he saw. He nourished his mind on what he looked at, as no one else was capable of looking. He put the most subtle intelligence into the act of watching, but that intelligence was heedless of everything except the creature who was being glowered at, pursued, held in sight, hunted down and trapped by his unwavering stare."

(continued on page 73)

Selected Works by
HENRI DE
TOULOUSE-LAUTREC

The Countess de Toulouse-Lautrec. Oil on canvas, 1882.

La Goulue Entering the Moulin Rouge. Oil on cardboard, 1892.

At the Moulin Rouge. Oil on canvas, 1892.

68   *Jane Avril at the Jardin de Paris.* Lithograph, 1893.

*Yvette Guilbert Taking
a Curtain Call.*
Gouache on cardboard, 1894.

69

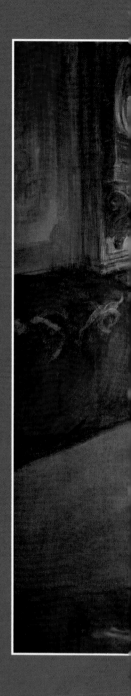

70

Dr. Gabriel Tapié de Céleyran.
Oil on canvas, 1894.

The Salon in the Rue des Moulins. Oil on canvas, 1894.

Marcelle Lender Dancing the Bolero. Oil on canvas, 1896.

(continued from page 64)

Beautiful women, rapid dancing, athletic movement, physical quirks, and telling gestures—Lautrec took these in through his dark, laughing eyes, processed them through his insightful mind, and reproduced them effortlessly (or so it seemed) on paper. It was not unusual for him to make a dozen or more sketches of a dancer's pose, a singer's comical expression, or a woman's delicate arms before committing them to canvas in his makeshift studio.

The young laundress who lived nearby on the rue Fontaine was one such subject who did not elude Lautrec's probing gaze. Her real name was Marie-Clémentine Valade, but she had taken the name Suzanne Valadon as a teenager when she had become a circus acrobat. As a result of a serious fall, however, she had been forced to retire and to earn a living as a laundress and a model for painters such as Renoir and Degas.

Though beautiful, Valadon was hardened by poverty and life on the streets. When she was not working to support her mother and three-year-old illegitimate son, she indulged in her secret habit of drawing and painting. Upon visiting her apartment, Lautrec spied her work and was immediately impressed. He found himself strongly attracted to Valadon and the two were soon romantically involved. Sylvia Horwitz wrote: "The guttersnipe and the count had a great deal in common. Marie was totally without prejudices. She had learned to look squarely at facts, to swallow what life served up, and to keep her own inner self fiercely private. Like Lautrec, she had intelligence and talent."

Their relationship was a stormy one. Valadon was temperamental and manipulative, and Lautrec, always vulnerable, suffered her moods in silence. After nearly two years of emotional ups and downs—including Valadon's faked suicide attempt—Lautrec left and vowed never to see her again. Ironically, Valadon went on to be a painter of

Everyone who met him seemed to have an opinion about Lautrec. A contemporary, Henry Van Der Velde, said, "Photographs of this little man have been seen all over the world. . . . In this stunted body there was an extreme vitality that almost went beyond Toulouse-Lautrec's spirit. His rapid wit, the wit of a malicious clown, was staggering. His mouth was of an animal sensuality, his way of talking now uncontrolled, now pointed and witty, now totally unconventional."

considerable merit. Today, her work hangs in museums around the globe, including the Louvre, which contains one of the richest collections of art in the world.

As in the aftermath of his first affair (with Marie Charlet), Lautrec drowned his disappointment in wine

Lautrec was obsessed with movement and, more often than not, depicted some sort of action in his work. At the Cirque Fernando: The Ring-master, *painted in 1888, illustrates Lautrec's interest in the graceful moves of circus performers and their animals.*

and work. He executed several excellent portraits during this time, which helped establish his name in the local Paris galleries. *The Drinker,* completed in 1889, depicts Valadon (she had posed for him before their breakup) sitting at a table with a glass of red wine, chin

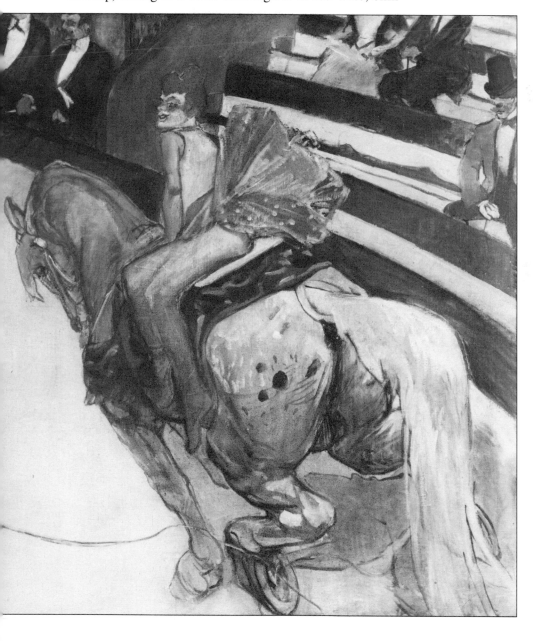

propped on her elbow, staring blankly into space. The portrait, which successfully conveys both the subject's beauty and her suffering, is one of Lautrec's most sensitive portraits. Also painted around the same time, *The First Communion* is a portrait of Lautrec's friend Gauzi and his family on their way to church. Without being judgmental, the work is a statement on the conformity and tedium of bourgeois life in late-19th-century Paris. "The gaunt, resigned father pushing the baby cart past the shirts in a laundry window, while the conventional little family trails behind" is how one writer described the painting. *Portrait of Hélène Vary* and *The Laundress* are both paintings of women (one a neighbor, the other a working girl) whose beauty, vulnerability, and tenderness are captured and held on Lautrec's canvas.

The artist's objectivity is apparent even in these early works. Unlike most of the portrait artists who preceded him—including Bonnat and Cormon—Lautrec made no judgments about his subjects, and therefore considered a portrait of a nobleman equal to that of a street vendor, and one of a prostitute the same as that of a princess. His artistic philosophy included the democratic idea that a portrait represented "the sum total of a life experience" and was not to be evaluated according to the social position of the subject.

"I am a painter of the streets," he later told his mother, who worried constantly about the toll his bohemian lifestyle would take on his already fragile health. But Lautrec's reassurances about his choice of occupation and relationships provided the countess with little comfort. In 1886, he had left the Greniers' home and moved in with fellow artist Henri Rachou. "Lack of space" was cited as one reason for the change, as was "the mental discomfort of living with a married couple." Lawrence and Elisabeth Hanson observed that "he was never again to live side by side with an intimacy he was unlikely to experience [himself]."

His arrangement with Rachou was short-lived as well. As Lautrec continued to push the limits of his art and experiment with new colors and techniques, his friend remained a traditional painter. When Rachou announced that he was engaged to be married, the scales were tipped once again. Lautrec then moved in with Dr. Henri Bourges, an old family friend whose apartment was in the same building as the Greniers'.

His next task was to find a studio of his own—a place that would afford him the privacy he needed to work and the space to store his materials, but with ready accessibility to his friends and colleagues. He found a suitable flat on the corner of rue Caulaincourt and rue Tourlaque and petitioned his parents for funds to cover the monthly rent. They agreed reluctantly, though it was apparent that nei-

Suzanne Valadon, with whom Lautrec was romantically involved, posed for this drawing, which was completed in 1889. The Drinker *shows a young woman sitting forlorn at a table in a bar and is considered to be one of Lautrec's most sensitive works.*

ther was pleased at the idea. Count Alphonse, like many Frenchmen of his class, counted Montmartre among the lowest rungs on the ladder of society. Countess Adèle, though supportive of her son's wishes, privately agonized over his choice of friends and lovers and his ever increasing consumption of alcohol. She consoled herself with the fact that Dr. Bourges would look after Henri's health and perhaps even persuade him, as she could not, to moderate his habits. Biographer Horwitz wrote: "She might have been less reassured had she . . . seen [his] studio. Its two outstanding features were dust and incredible disorder." It consisted of two rooms with a single entrance and included "a stunning display of bottles and all the accessories of a bar . . . an antique cabinet whose cluttered inside held everything from lacquered helmets, ballet shoes and old newspapers to Japanese scrolls, dumbbells and soda-water siphons. . . . And then there was the huge easel and a ladder nine feet high with ladies' headgear and clowns' hats strewn over the rungs. The model's table in the center of the room was littered with drawing materials, books, newspapers, tracing paper." Lautrec kept a rowing machine in the corner of the larger room, and despite his penchant for sitting, sketching, and drinking for hours at a time, he managed to keep himself physically fit.

The move to his own studio was not the only landmark in Lautrec's progression as a professional artist. In 1886, he accepted an invitation to exhibit at the Salon des Incohérents (Exhibition of the Incoherent Arts), a recently formed group of painters, sculptors, and caricaturists whose "sense of the absurd and satirical" was well known. Lautrec's entry was a Paris street scene, rue des Batignolles, entitled *Les Batignolles Three and a Half Years B.C. Painted in Oil on Emory Paper*. The plate underneath the painting identified the artist not as Lautrec, but as "Tolau-Segroeg, A Hungarian of Montmartre who has visited Cairo." At a subsequent exhibition by the Incohérents, he used the same pseudonym for his entry *Portrait of an*

Unfortunate Family Stricken with Pockmarks and described himself as a Montmartre painter "who lodges with one of his friends in the rue Yblas under the third gas-lamp on the left . . . specializing in family groups with yellow or pastel backgrounds." The exhibitions of the Incohérents afforded Lautrec the opportunity to show his work in a casual, nonjudgmental atmosphere. In effect, they were practice sessions for the more serious exhibitions to follow.

In 1888, when he was invited to show his work in Brussels, the capital of Belgium, at the Groupe des XX (Group of Twenty), Lautrec worked feverishly for weeks on end, selected 12 of his best paintings, and signed them in his own name. His entries garnered much praise by the critics who attended the exhibit. Vincent van Gogh's brother, Théo, an art dealer, took several of Lautrec's works for his own Paris gallery.

This exhibition was Lautrec's first major commercial success and signaled his formal entry into the art world. It would have been easy for him to become overconfident and boastful as a consequence of his initial achievement, but he chose to remain rather humble, self-critical, and hardworking. In a letter to his mother he wrote, "I am sending you a very generous article which has been published about me claiming that my work should have been more advantageously placed [at the exhibit]. . . . I have just finished [some] portrait[s]. . . . I hope they won't be considered too ugly."

Lautrec was gaining momentum as an artist. As the paint dried and the finished canvases accumulated in his studio, the inhabitants of Montmartre were busy discussing the grand opening of its newest entertainment attraction. And though Lautrec could not yet know it, the Moulin Rouge would provide him with the inspiration for some of his finest work and would play a major role in the development of his career.

This 1890 photomontage is entitled Monsieur Toulouse Painting Monsieur Lautrec Monfa. *At a later date, Paul Leclerq, a friend of Lautrec's, described what it was like to pose for him: "He would stare intently at me through his spectacles, screw up his eyes, reach for a paintbrush and, after studying carefully what he had been looking at, place a few strokes of . . . paint on his canvas. While he was painting he remained silent, and, licking his lips, seemed as though he was relishing something with a particularly exquisite taste."*

6

LES CAFÉS-CONCERTS

BEGINNING IN 1889 and continuing through the mid-1890s, scenes from Paris dance halls and cabarets became the focus of and inspiration for most of Lautrec's work. He frequented clubs such as Le Divan Japonais (The Japanese Room), Les Ambassadeurs (The Ambassadors), Alcazar (named after a town on the border of French and Spanish Morocco), Le Moulin Rouge (The Red Mill), and the Elysée-Montmartre (Montmartre Paradise), where he studied the patrons, the owners, and especially the performers with ever increasing interest. His boyhood fascination with sport and movement (expressed in his early sketches of hunting dogs, horses, and carriages) resurfaced in adulthood with his depictions of cabaret performers and dance hall entertainers.

La Goulue and her partner Valentin-le-Désossé were the first dance hall performers to capture Lautrec's attention. They were the subjects of countless sketches and provided the inspiration for Lautrec's first successful poster. In addition, one or both of them are pictured in several of his major paintings, including *At the Moulin de la Galette, At the Moulin Rouge, At the Moulin Rouge: The Dance,* and *La Goulue Entering the Moulin Rouge.*

It was during this time that the *quadrille naturaliste*— a group of four female cancan dancers known for their revealing high kicks and unparalleled flexibility—became the sensation of Paris. Everyone, it seemed, wanted to be part of the crowd when the quadrille was performing. "People poured in," wrote Lawrence and Elisabeth Hanson, "painters, poets, journalists, men about town, demimondaines [scandalous women], society women, roisterers, and royalty sitting table to table—to watch, to listen, drink, dance, but as time went on more and more to watch."

Le fin de siècle (the end of the century) had arrived with its increasing urbanization, modern inventions, and democratic ideals. There was an air of restlessness and confusion as Parisians and other Europeans alike struggled to cope with the rapid changes in day-to-day life brought on by advances in science, medicine, and technology. The World's Fair of 1889, which took place in Paris and was attended by Lautrec and his friends, served as a preview of the changes to come in the 20th century. The 984-feet-high steel Eiffel Tower—erected in close proximity to some of the oldest buildings in Paris—sparked a heated controversy between the modernists and traditionalists in Paris society. *La Tour Eiffel* seemed to underscore the fact that urban culture, with its fast-paced, pleasure-seeking, production-oriented value system, was destined to dominate Europe for decades to come.

For Lautrec, as for many people of the time, it was a combination of curiosity, escapism, and desire to insulate himself from events beyond his control that led him night after night to the cabarets of Montmartre. After the success of his first poster for the owners of the Moulin Rouge, the club remained Lautrec's favorite rendezvous and its performers continued to be his most cherished artistic subjects. Seated at his usual table toward the back of the main room, he filled sketch pad after sketch pad with dancers, tourists, bartenders, aristocrats, drunkards, and prostitutes. He developed a remarkable ability to concentrate on his work while surrounded by the constant noise and movement of this earthy yet exotic atmosphere. In their 1956 biography, Lawrence and Elisabeth Hanson described the Moulin Rouge as it must have appeared to Lautrec:

> The noise inside the hall was deafening; near the entrance the band could not be heard, its size and weight of brass notwithstanding, for the clapping, cheering, cries of dancers, talking, shrieking—for a quarrel was usually going on somewhere. . . . The atmosphere matched the noise. There was no ventilation and despite the height of the roof the dust from the floor boards and from the rice powder with which every woman's face was thickly coated, together with the moisture from the breath and perspiration of hundreds of people, formed a thick and steamy haze that dimmed the lights and clouded the mirrors. . . . [Yet] all this formed part of the enjoyment. . . . They were all having the time of their lives.

In January 1890, however, Lautrec "tore himself away for a few weeks" from the nightlife of Montmartre in order to exhibit at the Groupe des XX in Brussels. He had first exhibited there in 1888. Renoir, Degas, and van Gogh were also showing their artwork, although unlike Lautrec, they chose not to personally attend. Like his father, Lautrec had an affinity for foreign places and gladly traveled to Brussels to take part in the banquet that honored the exhibiting French and Belgian artists.

What began as a pleasant excursion, however, rapidly developed into an unpleasant situation. One of the Belgian artists, Henri de Groux (who was, ironically, a dwarf) drank excessively during the dinner and began slandering Vincent van Gogh in front of the other guests. It is not clear as to why de Groux disliked van Gogh, but because of his drinking, de Groux was more aggressive than usual. Lautrec, who had befriended van Gogh while studying at Cormon's studio, rose to his colleague's defense. (At this time, van Gogh was in a mental hospital at Saint-Rémy, and so was obviously unable to defend himself.) A heated argument ensued, culminating in Lautrec challenging de Groux to a duel. Fortunately for both men, the event never took place and de Groux's Belgian colleagues shamed him into apologizing.

The exhibit itself was a great success, however, for both Lautrec and van Gogh sold paintings there (the latter's only sale prior to his death in 1890) and received promising critical commentary.

Upon his return to Paris, Lautrec rekindled his interest in portraits, choosing as subjects members of the musical Dihau family. Marie Dihau was an accomplished pianist, and her brother, Désiré, was a bassoonist in the orchestra at the Paris Opera. When Lautrec produced gentle and sensitive portraits of them in 1890, he displayed "a friend's affection" in his work. He entered *Désiré Dihau Reading a Paper* and *Mademoiselle Dihau at the Piano* at the next exhibit at the Cercle Volney in Paris and again at the Salon des Indépendants. Both received the critics' approval.

Lautrec's formal training as a portrait artist had served him well. Among his many portraits, he had previously completed those of colleagues Émile Bernard, Henri Rachou, and Vincent van Gogh; and a female acquaintance Rosa the Redhead. However, he was totally incapable of suppressing his attraction to movement and performance, and before long he returned to his usual table at the Moulin Rouge.

It was the end of 1892, and the reign of La Goulue as the queen of the dance hall was drawing to a close. Her successor was Jane Avril, a woman who was the antithesis of La Goulue in personality, physique, and artistic style. She was only 20 years old when Moulin Rouge owner

Lautrec befriended the Dihau family, which included Marie, a pianist, and Désiré, a bassoonist at the Paris Opera, and proceeded to paint portraits of them. Shown here is Mademoiselle Dihau at the Piano, *completed in 1890.*

Charles Zidler hired her to perform. When Lautrec was first introduced to Avril and carefully studied her delicate features, he suspected that the dancer was no stranger to disappointment and suffering. His observations were confirmed when he learned that, as a young girl, Avril frequently had been abused by her mentally unbalanced mother and for a time had survived by begging in the streets. After several years of this way of life, the girl had been admitted to a mental hospital for treatment of hysteria and intense phobias (from which she never fully recovered) and took up dancing as a form of expressive therapy.

Upon her release, she sought to make a living as a dance hall performer.

Lautrec was intrigued by Avril's measured, graceful, almost intellectual dancing style and her quiet, humble demeanor. Her performances were a sharp contrast to those of La Goulue, whose boisterous manner and bold, uninhibited movements had once been the mainstay of the Moulin Rouge act. Avril's movements, on the other hand, were elegant, reserved, and almost apologetic. Yet, despite their artistic differences, she appeared no less popular with the crowds than her more outrageous predecessor.

Lautrec studied Avril for hours, completing numerous sketches and drawings with the dancer as his main subject. There was a palpable sadness in her style that fascinated the long-suffering Lautrec and endeared her to him both as an artist and a friend. Their relationship grew more intimate, and Avril often accompanied Lautrec to dinner, to the theater, on long carriage rides around the city, or to the local bars. Together, they silently bore the consequences of childhood misfortunes, hoping that professional success in their respective fields might somehow make up for years of frustration and unhappiness.

When Avril left the Moulin Rouge in search of a more sophisticated audience, Lautrec followed. He did three posters and several oil paintings of her, all of which served to augment her popularity as a performer. "There is no doubt," Avril later stated with characteristic humility, "that I owe my celebrity to him; it began after he made his first poster of me."

The next cabaret performer to capture Lautrec's interest was Yvette Guilbert. She was an unusual-looking woman whose only talent seemed to lie in the ability to squeak out simpleminded songs with verses containing scattered obscenities. "She was a tall, thin, young woman with a skinny neck and skinny arms, made to look even thinner with elbow-length black gloves," wrote Elisabeth and Lawrence Hanson. "Her face consisted of an immense mouth, a bulbous nose and a pair of black, hollow eyes. Her voice was acid, her hair was red . . . a red that cost her twenty-five francs a month."

In developing an interest in Guilbert, Lautrec once again displayed his love for paradox, humor, and absurdity. It took him longer, however, to embrace Guilbert's comic style and personality than it had Avril's more sophisticated one. He first pictured her in the background of a poster for the Divan Japonais nightclub. He then included her in an illustration for the Paris journal *Le Figaro,* but again without the idolization that had been so apparent with La Goulue and Jane Avril.

In 1894, however, Guilbert was the subject of no less than 16 of Lautrec's lithographs. Jean Bouret explained Lautrec's delay in using the singer as an inspiration for his work: "Lautrec was waiting for the subject to ripen in his mind. His first impression was usually right, but it was not until his brain had analyzed the model's features and events had confirmed that first impression, that the work would flower."

The public's reaction to the posters was favorable, and as in the case of Avril, helped to establish Guilbert's prominence in the Parisian entertainment world. Guilbert's own reaction to Lautrec's portrayals, however, was less favorable. "For the love of heaven," she wrote to him after viewing a preliminary sketch, "don't make me so astonishingly ugly!"

Lautrec had never intended the sketch to be a complimentary portrait, but rather "had merely followed her in emphasizing certain features . . . extracting from the whole woman the clown she deliberately produced in public," wrote Lawrence and Elisabeth Hanson. Though Lautrec remained a realistic painter throughout his career, his affinity for the absurd, humorous, and paradoxical (in Guilbert's case, a glamorous woman singing obscenities) would surface from time to time in the form of caricature.

This aspect of Lautrec's art figures prominently in two other works produced around this time. In executing his lithographic portrait of composer and club owner Aristide Bruant and his oil portrait of his cousin Gabriel Tapié de Céleyran, Lautrec used caricature to emphasize his subjects' physique and demeanor. Bruant's bulky torso and his overbearing, flamboyant personality are captured perfectly in posters made by Lautrec in 1892 and 1893. The influence of Japanese woodcuts—which he studied with increasing interest in the 1890s—shows itself clearly in

Aristide Bruant in His Cabaret *was created in 1892 to advertise a singing appearance of Lautrec's friend at a club called the Ambassadeurs. Bruant's large body and overwhelming personality are vividly captured in this lithograph.*

the clean lines, sharply contrasting colors, and flattened-image effects of *Aristide Bruant in His Cabaret* and *Bruant at the Mirliton.*

In the 1894 *Dr. Gabriel Tapié de Céleyran,* Lautrec paints an affectionate portrait of his relative who had come to Paris to study medicine and surgery under the celebrated Dr. Jules-Émile Péan. Céleyran afforded Lautrec a vital link to his past and to his family (Lautrec's father remained a distant, self-indulgent parent and had little to do with his son). He proved to be a loyal friend, though a somewhat reluctant nightclub companion: "He provided in every way precisely the contrast relished by Toulouse-Lautrec; he was an excessively thin young man and so tall that he walked with a permanent stoop; in opposition to the bold profile of his cousin he had the kind of face that slopes away in every direction, from long, thin nose to the slanting forehead and to the hairless receding chin," wrote biographers Lawrence and Elisabeth Hanson. "When they sat together . . . [it] caused extreme amusement in their friends. . . . The more unmercifully [Céleyran] was bullied by [Lautrec] the better he seemed to like it."

Despite Lautrec's insistence on leading his own life and pursuing the bohemian lifestyle of a Montmartre artist, he reveled in his cousin's companionship. Likewise, Céleyran took Lautrec's eccentric behavior, alcoholic overindulgences, and disreputable acquaintances in stride. In his own quiet way, he became an advocate of Lautrec's art, remarking constantly about his superior concentration, stamina, and perfectionism. Like many nonartists, Céleyran had wrongly assumed that painters took less time and care to produce a single picture than they actually did. He was amazed at the number of hours his cousin spent making preliminary drawings and sketches, preparing his subjects and materials, and putting the finishing touches on a painting or a poster.

Céleyran could only shake his head in disbelief as his cousin set off for the printer's shop early in the morning after a long night of drinking and sketching. Lautrec's boyhood friend Maurice Joyant remembered that after arriving at the shop and "after the expected jokes and a drink Lautrec would bend over the [lithograph] stone, working with such skill and earnestness that the [printer's] men were amazed and more than a little respectful. His clothes were, of course, his evening clothes, he having had no more than one of his cat naps at his studio."

Lautrec the professional was both "playful and determined." He developed a method of applying small areas of color to the lithographic stone and then scattering them over a wider area using various sized toothbrushes to obtain his *crachis* (dotted effect). "That the good poster is as it is today is due to Toulouse-Lautrec more than any other man," wrote Lawrence and Elisabeth Hanson. "He could reasonably be described as the founder of modern poster design and so one who, more than any other artist, has affected the lives of the people, since it is by way of the good poster that the art education of the people commonly begins."

Lautrec's prodigious production during the early to mid-1890s was due, in part, to his maturation as an artist and the continued praise for his posters from those who commissioned him.

But there were personal factors as well that contributed to his success. In 1893, his friend and roommate Henri Bourges was married, necessitating yet another move for Lautrec. Countess Adèle, who had not relinquished her hope of providing her son with a more stable lifestyle, seized the opportunity by offering to take an apartment nearby. Lautrec agreed and once again resided under his mother's roof, this time at 9, rue de Douai, Montmartre.

At about this same time, Lautrec's friend Joyant—who was now director of the renowned Goupil Gallery in Paris—arranged an exhibition that showcased Lautrec's work and that of painter-engraver Charles Maurin. It was Lautrec's first major exhibition in Paris and it received "fairly good press." The critics essentially liked his work but disapproved of the tawdriness of his subjects, however, a reaction that Lautrec had anticipated and to which he was growing more and more accustomed.

It was Degas's reaction that had the most positive impact on Lautrec's spirit, for Degas remained his idol and a somewhat distant mentor. Lawrence and Elisabeth Hanson described the master Impressionist's subtle but approving evaluation of the exhibit:

> [Degas] arrived late one afternoon swathed in a large overcoat and walked slowly around the room, examining the pictures closely and humming under his breath. He said nothing until he was halfway down the stairs on his way out; then he looked back for a moment to Toulouse-Lautrec, speechless with uncharacteristic nervousness, with a "Well, Lautrec, one can see that you belong to us."

The show was a success, and Joyant encouraged Lautrec to keep working and to guard his health. Maurice Joyant was to remain, throughout Lautrec's lifetime and several decades thereafter, an "undeviatingly loyal friend" as well as the most zealous advocate of Lautrec's art. He fought off those who criticized Lautrec's work because of its subject matter and educated those who underestimated the technical mastery required to produce his many posters and lithographs. Twenty years after the artist's death, it was Joyant who persuaded the French government to establish the Toulouse-Lautrec Museum in Albi, which today houses several hundred of Lautrec's drawings, sketches, paintings, and posters.

In 1894, Joyant asked his friend to accompany him to London on a business trip. Lautrec, like many sophisticated Parisians of that era, was an enthusiastic Anglophile and often imitated the English in dress, speech, mannerisms, and cuisine. Lautrec also had a penchant for the sea, a fondness that had grown during his many visits to health spas near the Mediterranean when he was

An Intern: Gabriel Tapié de Céleyran *is a drawing of Lautrec's cousin, whose physical characteristics were the complete opposite of Lautrec's. Biographers comment that friends were greatly amused when seeing the pair sitting together.*

Although the painting The Last Crumb *was posed, it shows a couple that Lautrec could have witnessed on any given day at one of the local cafés he frequented. The drunken bliss of the man and the melancholic mood of the woman are captured in this 1891 work, typical of Lautrec's realistic, intimate style.*

younger. These two factors combined to make Lautrec a most willing traveling companion, and he gladly accepted the invitation.

Joyant's intentions were twofold, however. He watched with increasing concern as Lautrec's eccentricities became more and more self-destructive and began to take a visible toll on the artist's health. Lautrec's long working hours, excessive drinking, and frequent visits to local brothels were disturbing to the more moderate Joyant, who had proposed the trip, in part, to remove Lautrec from these unhealthy temptations. In London, where the police were strict, he knew there would be little opportunity for Lautrec's drinking to get out of hand, and fewer chances for him to take up with prostitutes. Most important, however, the journey would give Lautrec a much needed rest, some fresh air, and a change of scenery, all of which Joyant hoped would revive Lautrec's once robust health.

On the day of departure, Lautrec appeared at the docks "carrying a long, thin yellow sausage of a bag—the only kind that in his hands would not scrape the ground," wrote Lawrence and Elisabeth Hanson. The artist, always cheerful despite his personal sufferings, was even more so during the rough crossing of the English Channel. He was childlike in his delight of the ship, the sea, and the waves and chattered endlessly with the crew and the other passengers. One of them recalled watching him as he "clung to the rail in an ecstasy, his head just clearing it, watching the waves, brushing his glasses down his overcoat with one hand, replacing them, staring ahead again and again, the glasses clouded by spray."

Upon their arrival in London, Joyant attended to his business for the Goupil Gallery while Lautrec took in the art museums, shops, and galleries and generally immersed himself in the English culture. The highlight of the journey was his meeting with Oscar Wilde, the celebrated writer and dramatist. Wilde, who was under investigation for alleged immorality, enjoyed his conversation with the Parisian painter but refused Lautrec's request that he pose for a portrait. Lautrec, at first gravely disappointed, decided later to do the painting anyway and based it on sketches he had made from memory. The result was, according to Lawrence and Elisabeth Hanson, "one of his cleverest portrait-caricatures."

But despite his Anglophile tendencies, Lautrec remained a true Frenchman at heart and grew tired of certain aspects of life in London. After a few weeks, he informed Joyant that "the formality, conventionality and hypocrisy" of the city were too much for him and that he was ready to go home. Joyant agreed, finished his appointments, and boarded the ship with his anxious friend.

Joyant was optimistic on the return voyage, observing that Lautrec's "remarkable constitution, though impaired, still responded almost immediately to fresh air and enforced sobriety." As he watched his friend joke with the crew and walk contentedly back and forth on the deck, he prayed that it would last.

Lautrec had become intensely interested in the theater and was commissioned to design a poster for a play, La Gitane, *that was opening in January 1900. Although the form is plainer than other lithographs he had created, it evokes drama simply by the depiction of the leading actress, dressed completely in white, who dominates the picture.*

7

NEW PERSPECTIVES

THE LAST HALF OF THE 1890s brought with it an increased restlessness as Europeans, including Parisians, anticipated the new century. It was a time of great innovation, when new ideas—spurred by a wave of scientific discoveries—led to inventions of products designed to make life easier, healthier, and more enjoyable.

The bicycle was one such invention. Frenchman Pierre Michaux had manufactured the first "velocipedes" in 1867, when Lautrec was just three years old. Since then, the bicycle had undergone several changes and improvements (including the change from wooden or metal wheels to American Charles Goodyear's rubber tires), resulting in a fun, affordable, and health-promoting vehicle. In the 1890s, bicycles became all the rage in Paris, their appeal successfully transcending class boundaries. Grocers, bartenders, and carpenters rode beside upper-class gentlemen, pedaling up and down the wide boulevards and steering cautiously through the narrow cobblestone alleyways.

Women took to the sport as easily as men, basking in the newfound freedom that the cycles provided. The more daring females raised eyebrows when they discarded their long, billowing dresses for more practical pants, beginning a fashion trend that was to remain for generations to come.

Lautrec watched the developing craze with great interest. As often as possible, he accompanied his friend Tristan Bernard to the velodrome (bicycle track) to watch the athletes train and compete in races of various distances. He felt at home there, and though he could not ride a bike himself, cycling became one of his favorite pastimes. Bernard, manager of the two most popular racing tracks in Paris and editor of a cycling newspaper, *Le Journal des Vélocipédistes,* permitted Lautrec access to the entire premises of the velodromes, including the showers and locker rooms, a privilege that enabled the artist to closely observe some of the country's most talented athletes.

As in the past, the objects of Lautrec's intense observation inevitably appeared in his sketches and on his posters. At the track, Lautrec seated himself comfortably on the infield grass and studied the cyclists as they raced, passing the spectators at dizzying speeds, their jerseys blurring into a rainbow of color. As they sped by, legs churning "like pistons" before the "yellow, flag-waving crowd," he drew them with the same enthusiasm as he had drawn the dancers at the Moulin Rouge.

Lautrec's drawings, which the athletes eagerly passed around, inspired the owners of the acclaimed Simpson bicycle chain to offer him a commission. Lautrec designed a poster in 1896 that he later deemed unsatisfactory, destroyed it, and designed a second one more to his liking. Louis "Spoke" Bouglé, the company's agent, was pleased, paid Lautrec his fee, and proceeded to use the poster in the company's newest promotional campaign. In France, it became one of Lautrec's most recognizable works and "was more lasting than the Simpson chain [itself]," according to biographer Horwitz.

La Chaîne Simpson

L.B. SPOKE
DIRECTEUR POUR LA FRANCE
25, Boulevard Haussmann.

During this time, Lautrec pursued other interests as well. On several occasions between the years 1894 and 1896, he took up residence in two of the better-known Paris brothels. There is much speculation among modern biographers as to his reasons for doing this, but all seem to agree that he did so for both personal and professional reasons. That he would never enjoy a conventional romance with a woman of his own class was quite apparent by this time, and he no doubt found warmth, affection, attention, and female companionship—which his friends and colleagues experienced with their wives or mistresses—in these infamous establishments. Biographer Jean Bouret went a step further in analyzing Lautrec's deep psychological needs: "[His] desire for a life lived in brothels . . . was an attempt to regain [the] warm atmosphere [of Le Bosc] . . . [a] shelter from the outside world."

When bicycles came into fashion in 1896, Lautrec made two posters for the Simpson chain, the second of which is seen here. He was unhappy with his first try, so Lautrec quickly produced another. The work became very popular throughout France and more well known than the bicycle company itself.

All written accounts of his life confirm that Lautrec—a passionate, intelligent, and highly sensitive man—thrived on the company of others, especially women. Unlike several prominent artists of his time who preferred to work in isolation (such as van Gogh and Gauguin), Lautrec abhorred prolonged periods of solitude. By living for weeks at a time in the brothels on the rue des Moulins and the rue d'Amboise, Lautrec guaranteed himself constant companionship, romance (for a price), and a little respect. "Within those special walls," wrote Sylvia Horwitz, "he was 'M'sieur Henri' to everybody. His every comfort was seen to. Nobody mocked him, and he in turn treated everyone with courtesy and kindness."

Lautrec, who was perhaps one of the greatest chroniclers of the fin de siècle period, also chose to inhabit the brothels in order to study and paint an important part of

Lautrec spent much of his time in the Paris brothels, and even lived in them between 1894 and 1896. The Two Friends, *painted in 1895, depicts a tender scene between two prostitutes.*

the metropolitan culture of the time. It was an aspect of life that was alternately ignored and condemned by high-class society, yet no one could deny that brothels had existed and thrived in Paris for centuries and that their influence on city life would no doubt continue well into the next one. Biographers Philippe Huisman and M. G. Dortu explain:

> His visits to the brothels and his periods of residence there were not the outcome of a sudden whim. He wished . . . to immerse himself completely in the life of these establishments, to be more than a mere tourist in a 'country' of which he ardently wished to convey a true picture. . . . Like [his contemporaries] Gauguin and van Gogh, he endeavored to grasp the reality and essence of alien surroundings . . . [but unlike them] his explorations were restricted to familiar ground.

In contrast to other men of his class, Lautrec made no attempt to hide the fact that he spent a considerable amount of time with prostitutes, and in fact, he seemed to enjoy the reactions of his friends when he confessed his habit. "He was highly amused by the bourgeois dread of houses of ill-fame," wrote Jean Bouret. "He thought it a great joke to invite [the art dealer] Durand-Ruel to visit him in the rue des Moulins when the dealer was about to arrange an exhibition. . . . The dismay evinced by [Durand-Ruel] on finding himself in the Salon among a bunch of lightly-clad ladies was well worth seeing."

His family, by now painfully aware of Lautrec's interest in brothel life, was not amused. "For the honor of the [family] name," declared Count Alphonse, who was still roaming from place to place in search of pleasure and sport, "it would be better if he chose his models elsewhere." Uncle Charles, who had supported Lautrec's artistic ambitions from the beginning, now found himself equally dismayed by his nephew's behavior. He ordered nearly a dozen of Lautrec's paintings that had been sent to Albi for storage to be burned. Though he knew that the art was masterful, Uncle Charles considered the subject matter "indecent" and showed no remorse at the paintings' destruction.

Whatever his motivation, it is clear that Lautrec felt compelled to extensively record the lifestyle and character of the brothel inmates. He believed that the women, though less visible than cabaret performers, dancers, and club owners, exerted an equal influence on Parisian society. "Among the large bourgeois section of the population . . . idleness prevailed," wrote Huisman and Dortu. "Its members hardly knew how to occupy long evenings and interminably long days insufficiently punctuated by . . . obligations [and] they became prey to boredom. . . . No one cared to contemplate the closing of the brothels, which paradoxically helped to preserve family unity . . . [and supplied] the sense of escape to unexplored worlds."

While in residence in the rue des Moulins, Lautrec completed more than 50 paintings and dozens of sketches and drawings that some critics claim to be his best work. In several of these, Degas's influence is evident. Lautrec shared Degas's fascination with women in relaxed poses, engaged in their work, or in simple, routine activities. But whereas Degas painted ballerinas tying their slippers, stretching their muscles, or resting after a performance, Lautrec painted prostitutes bathing, dressing, combing their hair, and awaiting a routine medical examination. He sketched them as they ate, slept, played endless games of cards, washed their clothes, and waited for their clients.

In 1896, he published an album of 10 lithographs entitled *Elles* (The Girls) in which he portrays the life of prostitutes with objectivity and tenderness. They include works such as *The Toilette, Woman at the Tub, Solitude,* and *Slumber.* Public reaction to the series was, as Lautrec anticipated, largely unfavorable. But some in the art world recognized the album as a masterpiece that contained "triumphant examples of observation and draftsmanship." To those who knew him well, *Elles* was a statement of

Lautrec's artistic philosophy, one that encompassed objectivity, realism, and the existence of beauty in all things. "The naturalness and spontaneity of these women, to whom nakedness was habitual, imbued them with a grace reminiscent of that of the nymphs and goddesses of antiquity," wrote Huisman and Dortu. "For Lautrec, beauty was inherent in life, in movement, in the absence of physical or moral restraint, and he wished to indicate the unquestionable superiority of the prostitutes in this respect over other women."

After making a thorough study of the brothels, Lautrec turned again to public performers as an inspiration for his work. Performance of any sort—be it horseback riding, cycling, dancing, acting, or singing—had always intrigued Lautrec, and his paintings treated these art forms with equal respect. To this list of his revered subjects, he now added several from a new arena, that of Le Nouveau Cirque (New Circus). When Lautrec was seven years old, his father had taken him to the circus for the first time, and it was there that his fascination for performers had begun. Later, Lautrec attended the circus with his art tutor René Princeteau who especially had admired the trained horses and their skilled equestrians. As an apprentice at Cormon's studio, Lautrec had become a regular audience member at performances of Le Cirque Fernando in Paris. *At the Cirque Fernando: The Ringmaster* (1888), which took him two years to complete, was his first major oil painting and eventually hung in the foyer of the Moulin Rouge.

At this time in his life, Lautrec rekindled his interest in the circus. For a while, he attended Le Nouveau Cirque nearly as often as he had frequented the Moulin Rouge when Jane Avril was performing. As his penetrating gaze dissected every move of the acrobats, clowns, equestrians, and jugglers, his pencil recorded them for future generations. "Lautrec was their passionate admirer and friend," wrote Horwitz. "He liked these nomads, whose customs and way of life singled them out from other men. He

The Clowness Cha-U-Kao *was one of Lautrec's most famous oil paintings portraying a circus performer, a star of Le Nouveau Cirque. Around 1896, when this painting was completed, Lautrec regained interest in the circus—he had initially been introduced to it by his first art tutor, René Princeteau.*

respected the zeal with which they worked to perfect their art."

Footit the clown was one of Lautrec's favorite performers. He was a master of improvisation and entertained Paris audiences night after night with his hilarious pantomimes. To the untrained eye, his act seemed nothing more than a series of outrageous tumbling feats combined with a number of comical poses. But Lautrec understood, as few others did, the skill and practice that lay behind even the simplest gesture. His deep respect for Footit's craft (and that of his partner Chocolat) is reflected in the dozens of drawings he made of him: "Every fleeting expression on his plaster-white face with the down-cornered mouth had purpose," wrote Horwitz. "Lautrec, that student of faces, sought out his secrets relentlessly. The sketches piled up."

The equally talented female clown Cha-U-Kao became Lautrec's next subject, and he made nearly as many sketches of her as he had of Footit. *The Clowness Cha-U-Kao,* which now hangs in the Louvre and is one of his most masterful oil paintings, shows the muscular performer in a relaxed pose as she recovers from a strenuous acrobatic performance.

By the end of the 1890s, Lautrec seemed to have exhausted his supply of subjects in the cabarets, dance halls, and circus arenas, and he turned his interest to the more refined and sophisticated realm of the theater. He became an avid fan of the stage, from the traditional to the avant-garde.

With her subtle grace and artistic poise, singer-actress Marcelle Lender was the first theater performer to capture Lautrec's attention. "He found her fascinating," wrote Jean Bouret. "He liked her rather prominent nose, her rather plump chin, the heavily made-up eyes which gave her the appearance of a girl from a brothel, her tawny hair. . . . He immediately made five lithographs of her."

Lender's flowing, athletic style was accentuated by the new kind of stage lighting that emanated from the floor upward, rather than from the ceiling downward as in the cabarets. These footlights gave Lender and her contemporary Loïe Fuller (whose illustrious scarf dance—standing still while moving long veils attached to her dress—drew huge crowds to the Folies-Bergère) an ethereal quality that Lautrec managed to capture on canvas. One of his fine paintings, *Marcelle Lender Dancing the Bolero,* portrays the actress in a pose that, according to Horwitz, is "startlingly beautiful. She has just come to rest after a fiery whirl, with one leg gracefully pointed. . . . Her petticoats refuse to subside; they seem to be foaming from her spin. . . . [She appears] as exotic as an orchid."

In addition to sketches, posters, and paintings of Lender, Fuller, and other prominent stage personalities, Lautrec designed sets for the experimental Théâtre de l'Œuvre, illustrated numerous play programs, and helped establish a new periodical for theater patrons called *L'Escarmouche* (The Skirmish).

His interest in the theater world was soon matched by a curiousity of the literary world, and his acquaintances therein provided additional inspiration for his art. Like many of his contemporaries, Lautrec was drawn into the social circle of publisher Thadée Natanson and his wife, Misia, who counted among their friends the most prominent painters, poets, novelists, playwrights, and actors of the day. Names such as Stéphane Mallarmé, Claude Debussy, Romain Coolus, Émile Zola, and Marcel Proust were invited to their frequent dinner parties as well as their more informal social gatherings.

As the editor and cofounder of the progressive newspaper *La Revue Blanche,* Thadée Natanson provided a forum for some of the most talented and controversial thinkers and writers in late-19th-century France. Lautrec furnished the newspaper with a steady stream of illustrations and quickly became a favorite of both the editor and his wife. "[Lautrec] knew how to make himself loved," wrote Thadée. "[He was] a creature of childlike weakness and amiability to whom one had not the heart to refuse anything. He was both imperious and tender, imposing his opinions, feelings, and wishes on all of us by dint of grace and obstinacy: in short, a beloved little tyrant."

The lovely, artistic, and highly social Misia Natanson found the artist "charming and droll" and "kept him at her side like an affectionate clown." Lautrec adored Misia, although because she was married, their relationship remained platonic.

Over the next few years, Lautrec became a surrogate member of the Natanson family, which included Thadée's two brothers Alfred and Alexandre. At the "grand open-

Lautrec vacations with Thadée and Misia Natanson at the seaside. Lautrec became good friends with the Natansons, often staying at their country home for extended visits, where he would picnic, go swimming and walking, and listen to Misia play the piano in the evenings.

ing" of Alexandre's apartment, Lautrec was designated as the honorary bartender, a post to which he was wonderfully suited and anxious to serve. The occasion "was one of the most glittering the city had ever known, graced by guests of outstanding literary and artistic talents." For once, Lautrec abstained totally from drinking and concentrated his efforts on providing the guests with new and delicious cocktails of his own creation (some historians attribute the introduction of the American cocktail in France directly to Lautrec). The ingredients in these concoctions were as potent as they were palatable, and by the party's end, their effects were obvious, wrote biographers Huisman and Dortu: "When morning came most of the three hundred guests lay in a drunken stupor, while Lautrec, who had refrained completely from drink, departed, serene and dignified, from the scene of his exploits, proud of the two thousand drinks he had dispensed."

Toward the end of Lautrec's short life, he lived with his mother, Adèle, at Malromé, where she could care for him.

8

THE DECLINE

LAUTREC'S ABSTENTION FROM ALCOHOL did not last long, and by the end of 1897 there were visible signs that his years of hard drinking and frequent visits to brothels (he eventually contracted syphilis, a contagious disease transmitted by sexual contact, for which there was no known cure) had precipitated both a physical and mental decline. He was uncharacteristically irritable, quarreled often with his friends, and seemed convinced that the police were pursuing him. His work output decreased, and he often interrupted portrait sittings for a necessary café visit to calm his trembling hands.

Ironically, though he drove many of his acquaintances away with his rude behavior and increasingly slovenly appearance, he was more afraid than ever of being left alone. According to biographer Jean Bouret, during an attack of delirium tremens (hallucinations caused by alcoholism), Lautrec saw "huge spiders in his room and had fired at them with a revolver, sobbing as he did so."

Ever faithful friend Maurice Joyant once again arranged for Lautrec to join him on a trip, this time to Brussels and then to the Loire Valley in France. Although the vacation provided Lautrec with a few weeks of fresh air, much needed rest, and a temporary distraction from the bars and brothels of Montmartre, it did little to improve his overall health.

Greatly concerned about his friend's physical decline and his lack of interest in painting, Joyant immediately arranged a one-man exhibition of Lautrec's work at the Goupil Gallery in London. The gesture backfired, however, as the critics gave it harsh reviews, claiming that Lautrec's sole intention was to showcase vice and debauchery. Fortunately, the prince of Wales felt differently, and when he purchased an oil painting of La Goulue, Lautrec was partially redeemed in the eyes of the London public.

Upon returning to Paris, Lautrec accepted a commission to illustrate Jules Renard's *Histoires Naturelles,* a book about natural history. Somehow he summoned the energy from his ravaged body to produce 28 drawings, mostly of animals, which received the overwhelming approval of both the author and publisher. Although it was critically acclaimed, the book was not a commercial success, and it represented Lautrec's last foray into book illustration.

Despite this brief surge of creativity, Lautrec was clearly on the decline. This was obvious to the artist himself ("There is no use denying that," he would say) and to all those who knew him. His friends implored him to drink more moderately and to stay away from the brothels, but their advice was disregarded. In February 1899, Lautrec collapsed in a Paris brothel. Several of the women there took him to his studio and summoned Lautrec's old friend, Dr. Bourges. Bourges looked after him as best he could, but when Lautrec remained "completely unconscious of his surroundings," the doctor knew that more help was needed. After consulting with Countess Adèle and Joyant, Bourges admitted Lautrec to a mental hospital in Neuilly.

In the weeks that followed, Lautrec was in the care of a team of doctors and nurses who specialized in the detoxification process, that is, ridding the body of foreign substances. Gradually, his body recovered and some of his former energy was restored. As the alcohol left his system, his speech became clearer, his memory more lucid, and his outlook increasingly cheerful.

As he improved both physically and mentally, his foremost concern was to expedite his return to the real world. Lautrec's personal freedom was his most cherished possession, and like his father, he was terribly afraid of confinement (the count had once said that whatever is robbed of its freedom withers away and dies). When he realized that the gift of independence hinged on the full recovery of his mental faculties and his total abstention from alcohol, he took pains to show everyone that he was a cured man. "It occurred to him that if he could again become the painter he used to be and proved it by his drawing," wrote Bouret, "the doctors would be bound to let him go."

Once this solution had taken root in the artist's mind, he requested some drawing paper and set to work. He executed—entirely from memory—39 drawings on circus themes, using, according to Bouret, "whatever materials came to hand—colored crayons, Indian ink, pastel, red chalk and pencil."

Meanwhile, the Paris press was having a field day with Lautrec's incarceration. A reporter from *Le Journal* wrote: "It was bound to end like this. . . . [Lautrec] has been shut up, and now madness, tearing off its mask, will place its official signature on the paintings, drawings and posters in which it has so long been anonymously present." Another journalist, Edmond le Pelletier, wrote in *L'Echo de Paris:* "[Lautrec] is to be found nowadays [in] a padded cell in a lunatic asylum."

In 1899 while vacationing with his chaperon, Paul Viaud, in Le Havre, Lautrec completed Englishwoman at The Star, Le Havre. *It was a painting of Miss Dolly, a blonde waitress in a seaport bar whom he had found captivating. He sent the work to Maurice Joyant, most likely to prove that although his health was poor, he could still paint.*

His friends and family, outraged at the lies being printed, invited art critic Arsène Alexandre from *Le Figaro* to visit the painter at Neuilly and write an article based on his observation. The critic agreed and on March 20, 1899, proclaimed:

> I saw a lunatic full of wisdom, an alcoholic who no longer drinks, a stricken man who never looked healthier. There is so much vitality in this supposedly dying man, such an innate strength in this supposedly sick creature that those who watched him hurrying to disaster are astonished to see him so splendidly restored to health.

On May 20, doctors pronounced Lautrec fit to leave the hospital, provided that he be accompanied everywhere by his chaperon, Paul Viaud. "M'sieur Viaud," as Lautrec called him, was a distant family relative from Bordeaux, a teetotaler, tactful, and understanding. He accompanied Lautrec to Paris where the painter renewed his social ties with the musical Dihau family and the literary Natanson clan. These friends, though happy to have the painter among them once again, remained concerned about his health. In spite of Lautrec's obvious sobriety, they noticed that he looked considerably "older [and] thinner," but they "didn't ask any questions."

Summer brought the usual seaside vacation and its welcomed diversions of sailing, swimming, and sunbathing. Viaud and Lautrec went to Bordeaux and to Le Havre, on the banks of the English Channel, where Lautrec painted an admirable portrait in red chalk of a waitress entitled *Englishwoman at The Star, Le Havre.*

In the fall, Lautrec returned to Paris refreshed, "in the pink of health," and determined to work. His newfound sobriety seemed to have rejuvenated him, and this was immediately reflected in his work. He reverted to the subjects that had fascinated him during his years at Le Bosc—namely, horses, riders, and their trainers. He produced several lithographs with horse racing themes that were skillfully executed and commercially successful. The profitable aspect of his work had only recently become important for Lautrec, because his family had curtailed his formerly generous monetary allowance.

For a while, Viaud's presence and Lautrec's low funds (which he often squandered in bars and brothels) effectively deterred his bad habits. However, for reasons that are unclear even today, Lautrec gradually returned to his old ways. Certainly it was much more difficult for Viaud to keep a watchful eye on the painter's kinetic energy in metropolitan Paris than it had been in Le Havre, a quiet seaside town. Once Lautrec was reinstated in his old surroundings, with access to his favorite cafés and nightclubs, the temptation to drink increased tenfold. His weakness was encouraged by a rare find in a Montmartre antique shop: a hollowed-out cane, which he promptly purchased and filled with liquor whenever his chaperon's attention wandered. "There was nothing the unsuspecting Viaud could do but worry," wrote Sylvia Horwitz. "He noticed the painter was having more difficulty walking . . . his hands trembled . . . he was visibly tired . . . it was getting harder and harder for him to climb the stairs to his bedroom. As the December nights grew longer, [Lautrec's] strength for nocturnal wandering diminished. The cab drivers who used to help him into the back seat of the carriage wondered what had happened to the little man whose tongue was so quick and whose tips were so generous."

In April 1900, more than 50 million people came to the World Exhibition in Paris, which ushered in a new century with exhibits from nations on nearly every continent. Lautrec was a member of the jury for the lithograph display, but he attended in a wheelchair, pushed alternately by several of his closest friends. For their sakes, he tried to appear interested and cheerful, but he was growing physically weaker with each passing day. He seldom painted, and when he did it took him many more sittings to finish than it had when he was Cormon's apprentice. He did manage to complete a few portraits, including those of playwright Romain Coolus, friend and art dealer Maurice Joyant, and his close friend Renée Vert.

When winter came, Lautrec decided to leave Paris and travel to Bordeaux, where he stayed for the remainder of the season. There, he frequently attended the opera to see productions of *La Belle Hélène* and *Messalina,* two of his favorites. He rented a small studio so he could paint the show's leading ladies and later sent the finished paintings to Joyant in Paris. Yet, as biographers Lawrence and Elisabeth Hanson point out, painting was not the only activity that filled Lautrec's time: "He not only worked hard at Bordeaux, he drank hard and slipped off night after night to the brothels . . . for the last month of 1900 and in the early months of 1901 he lived, the anxious, alarmed, protesting Viaud notwithstanding, much as he had lived in Paris for so many years before his breakdown. But he was no longer the man who could work and play at a stretch without apparent effect. His recovery . . . had been too quick to be true."

In February 1901, Lautrec suffered a partially paralyzing stroke. Fortunately, his brain was not affected, and with a combination of his mother's care and the application

Lautrec made many lithographs with the theme of horses at the racetrack. The Jockey, *printed in 1899, is considered to be one of Lautrec's finest lithographs and it embodies the love for horses that he inherited from his family.*

*Lautrec influenced a great
many artists with his unique
style and untraditional subject
matter. One such artist was
Édouard Vuillard, who
captured his friend on canvas
in this painting,* Portrait of
Henri de Toulouse-Lautrec,
in 1897.

of the new electric shock treatment, he recovered. He
knew, however, that it was only a matter of time until his
system collapsed completely, and this realization forced
him into action. His only concern became returning to his
Montmartre studio to put his affairs in order.

In April 1901, Viaud and Lautrec left Bordeaux and
returned to Paris. Upon his arrival, Lautrec immediately
made a thorough inventory of his paintings, sketches, and
lithographs, straightened his studio (a daunting task),
signed his name to all of his finished compositions,
and discarded those works that were unfinished or other-
wise unsatisfactory.

By July, he felt that his work in Montmartre was completed. He left Paris by train on July 15, after receiving an affectionate and tearful farewell from his closest friends. Accompanied by Viaud, Lautrec journeyed to the seaside resort at Taussat, in a last effort to regain some of his former strength.

The attempt failed, however, and a month later he was almost completely paralyzed by another stroke, the inevitable outcome of progressive syphilis. His mother came to Taussat immediately and took him to Malromé where she could watch over him and care for him in his last days.

According to Lawrence and Elisabeth Hanson, by this time, Lautrec was "a mere shadow of himself" and almost totally incapacitated. Nevertheless, he demanded a brush and paints so that he could finish his portrait of Paul Viaud. Because the unfinished painting hung above the mantel in the dining room, he painted while lying on a platform that family members and servants hoisted high above their heads. When they urged him to give up the task and rest, he simply laughed. "All my life I've never been anything but a pencil," he told them.

On September 9, 1901, not yet 37 years old, Henri de Toulouse-Lautrec Monfa died. For the most part, his death went unnoticed and unmourned. But for those who had known him well, who had recognized his genius and had forgiven his weaknesses, the loss was almost too much to bear. It was only in remembering Lautrec's own words that they were somewhat comforted. "Life is beautiful," he used to say, "[but] one must learn to bear with oneself."

The Toilette, *an 1896 oil painting by Lautrec, sold for $3.5 million in 1991.*

EPILOGUE

IMMEDIATELY FOLLOWING LAUTREC'S DEATH, several French newspapers published erroneous accounts of his demise, seeking to discredit both the artist and his work: "Henri de Toulouse-Lautrec has just died in a nursing-home, after violent attacks of insanity, after a terrible, vigorous struggle for healing," wrote le Pelletier in *L'Echo de Paris*. "Three years ago already he had been shut up, but afterwards was able to emerge from the horrible house of madmen. . . . Among the painters of his day he will leave traces of his curious, bad talent, the talent of a deformed creature who saw everything around him as ugly and exaggerated the ugliness of life." Curiously enough, his family did not respond to this article or to others, choosing instead to remain silent and allow time to erase unwanted memories and to mollify the antagonistic sentiments of Paris journalists. Lautrec's unsold paintings and prints remained in the possession of his family

and friends, and his existence was gradually forgotten by
the Paris public.

European society in the early 1900s, decadent and experimental though it was, maintained an air of dignity and
propriety. The pleasure seekers (of whom there were
many) were forced to conduct their affairs behind a facade
of tradition and politeness. Because this widespread hypocrisy precluded the acceptance of scandalous subject
matter in the visual arts, Lautrec's work remained generally scorned.

As the 20th century progressed, however, behavioral
taboos disappeared and artistic traditions were left behind
in the advance of technology and scientific discovery.
Biographer Jean Bouret wrote: "[These] years saw the
emergence of a rationalistic man, believing in the virtues
of science . . . a man who had shaken off the trammels
of religion . . . [who] conceive[d] the possibility of a
freedom that earlier custom would have completely [dis-
allowed]."

This liberation of values, ideas, and behaviors opened
up the door for the acceptance of new art forms and modes
of human expression. Consequently, Lautrec's work fell
into increasing favor with the public, and by 1914, Maurice
Joyant was arranging the first major retrospective exhibition of Lautrec's art. The honesty and realism apparent
in his work—aspects that were formerly dismissed or
overlooked—could now be appreciated by a more open-
minded public. Observed Bouret:

> Lautrec was . . . a rationalist. When he draws a prostitute
> taking some odious-looking customer upstairs he is not
> proffering an indictment of the bourgeois [preying] on a
> poor misguided girl—he just happens to have seen, on that
> particular day, a man with that particular face. Indeed, this
> truthfulness is really what some of his contemporaries
> found unpardonable! . . . Lautrec shows life as he saw and
> experienced it . . . he describes [people] as a naturalist
> describes insects, [individuals] caught at any hour of the

day and who are not posing, in other words not changing
the slightest detail, the smallest facial expression.

Joyant outlived Lautrec by 29 years, and during that
time he remained the artist's most faithful supporter. He
zealously refuted the harsh obituaries, defending both Lautrec's character and his art against critics who labeled it
too shallow or too commercial. With the help of Countess
Adèle, he promoted Lautrec's paintings and lithographs,
selling them through his own Paris gallery and helping to
stage exhibitions elsewhere in France. In 1902, he organ-
ized an exhibition of 200 items at the prestigious Durand-
Ruel gallery. That same year, the countess donated 371
lithographs to the Bibliothèque Nationale (National Library of France) in Paris, and in 1907 she helped Joyant
arrange a Lautrec exhibition in Toulouse. Count Alphonse
was less supportive, however, actively opposing a group
that planned to erect a statue in Lautrec's honor and
forbidding one writer to publish his son's biography.

The year 1914 was an auspicious one. Although the
Lautrec exhibition in Paris was shortened by France's
entry into World War I, the paintings *The Clowness Cha-
U-Kao* and *Woman at Her Toilette* were purchased by the
Luxembourg Museum. During the 1920s and 1930s, Lautrec's work "withstood the vagaries of auction sales with
notable success," wrote biographers Huisman and Dortu,
as several of the most prominent collectors of the early
20th century became intrigued with his style and subject matter.

As the value of both the prints and paintings increased,
Joyant worked tirelessly to ensure that Lautrec's greatness
was fully recognized. He compiled a two-volume biography of Lautrec, *Henri de Toulouse-Lautrec* (1926–27),
cataloged all of his paintings, sketches, and prints, and
convinced the French government to dedicate the Palais
de Berbie (the artist's birthplace) as a Lautrec museum.
Throughout 1922, its inaugural year, the museum had

2,300 visitors. Over the next four decades, attendance increased to nearly 40,000 annually. Today, each year, more than 100,000 people pass through the rooms and hallways of the Toulouse-Lautrec Museum in Albi where more than 600 sketches, posters, and paintings are displayed.

Gradually, Lautrec's influence spread beyond the boundaries of his beloved country. When Joyant died in 1930, he had successfully established his friend among the great French artists of his time. After World War II, Lautrec's paintings and posters sold at international public auctions for tens of thousands of dollars. By the mid 1960s, his oil paintings and lithographs were represented in museums in North and South America, Europe, and Asia. Today, in the United States, Lautrec's work can be seen in leading museums such as the Art Institute of Chicago, the National Gallery in Washington, D.C., and the Metropolitan Museum of Art in New York.

Joseph Rishel, curator of the Philadelphia Museum of Art (home of *At the Moulin Rouge: The Dance,* one of Lautrec's finest oil paintings), considers Lautrec "one of the most enchanting artists who ever lived. He possessed a poetic vision of humanity," states Rishel, "and concerned himself primarily with individuals, people in 'the theater of life.' . . . Had he lived in modern times, he would have loved the video camera [because] his interest lay primarily in human encounters. Lautrec was one of the first to blur the line between commercial and artistic activity."

Édouard Vuillard (1868–1940), a French artist whose work was influenced by Lautrec's, commented, "I was always struck by the way Lautrec changed his way of talking when art was being discussed. On any other subject he was cynical and witty, but on art he became totally serious. It was like a religious belief for him."

Other 20th-century artists such as Hans Hofmann (1880–1966), Pablo Picasso (1881–1973), Jackson Pol-

lock (1912–56), and Andy Warhol (1928–87) were also influenced by Lautrec's style, choice of subjects, and precise drafting technique. The flattened images that Lautrec employed in his lithographs are considered pre-cursors of Cubism, the modern geometric representation with which Picasso is most often associated. After visiting the Toulouse-Lautrec Museum in Albi, acclaimed poet and art enthusiast Jaime Gil de Biedma said, "It is curious to observe what Picasso became thanks to him, and one asks if there would have been room for this development if Lautrec had not died at [36] years of age."

Like many of Lautrec's works, The Bed *was criticized for its subject matter of two prostitutes lying in bed when it was painted in 1896, but is now critically acclaimed and extremely valuable.*

Today, the assessed value of Lautrec's work continues to rise. His lithographs are worth between $5,000 and $75,000 apiece, depending on the condition of the print and the total number produced in its original series. At prestigious auction houses such as Christie's and Sotheby's, Lautrec's oil paintings command prices ranging from $100,000 to more than $1 million each. (In 1991, for example, *The Bed* sold for $1.93 million, and *La Toilette* for $3.5 million.)

But the true value of Lautrec's art cannot be expressed in numbers alone. His legacy of talent, determination, sacrifice, and technical innovation continues to be an inspiration to artists in many different fields worldwide. The eminent Italian filmmaker Federico Fellini (1920–93) counted himself among those who drew inspiration from Lautrec's life and work. He wrote, "I have never looked with indifference at a painting, a poster, or a lithograph by Lautrec, and thoughts of him have seldom been far from my mind. Here was an aristocrat who disliked high society, who believed that the finest and purest flowers sprouted in wasteland and rubbish heaps . . . he detested hypocrisy and artifice. He was simple and true, magnificent despite his physical [disability]. For this reason Lautrec lives on, thanks to his pictures, in the heart of each of us."

FURTHER READING

Arnold, Matthias. *Henri de Toulouse-Lautrec.* Translated by Michael Hulse. Köln, Germany: Benedikt Taschen Verlag, 1992.

Bouret, Jean. *Court Painter to the Wicked: The Life and Work of Toulouse-Lautrec.* New York: Abrams, n.d.

Castleman, Riva, and Wolfgang Wittrock. *Henri de Toulouse-Lautrec: Images of the 1890s.* New York: The Museum of Modern Art, 1985.

Denvir, Bernard. *Toulouse-Lautrec.* New York: Thames and Hudson, 1991.

Dortu, M. G., and Philippe Huisman. *Toulouse-Lautrec.* New York: Doubleday, 1973.

Durozoi, Gerard. *Toulouse-Lautrec.* New York: Crescent Books, 1992.

Hanson, Lawrence, and Elisabeth Hanson. *The Tragic Life of Toulouse-Lautrec.* New York: Random House, 1956.

Horwitz, Sylvia. *Toulouse-Lautrec: His World.* New York: Harper & Row, 1973.

Julien, Édouard. *Toulouse-Lautrec.* Translated by Helen C. Slonim. New York: Crown, 1991.

Lassaigne, Jacques. *Toulouse-Lautrec and the Paris of the Cabarets.* New York: Hippocrene Books, 1970.

Lucie-Smith, Edward. *A Concise History of French Painting.* New York: Praeger, 1971.

Novotny, Fritz. *Toulouse-Lautrec.* New York: Greenwich House, 1983.

O'Connor, Patrick. *Nightlife of Paris: The Art of Toulouse-Lautrec.* New York: Universe, 1991.

Reuss, Henry, and Margaret Reuss. *The Unknown South of France.* Boston: The Harvard Common Press, 1991.

Roboff, Ernest. *Henri de Toulouse-Lautrec.* New York: Doubleday, 1969.

Russell, John. *Paris.* New York: Abrams, 1983.

CHRONOLOGY

1864   Henri Marie Raymond de Toulouse-Lautrec Monfa is born in Albi, France, on November 24

1867   Henri's brother, Richard, is born, but later dies in infancy

1872   Henri moves to Paris with his parents and attends the Lycée Fontanes

1874   The Toulouse-Lautrecs return to Albi because of Henri's physical frailty and ill health

1878   Henri fractures left thigh bone while getting out of a chair

1879   Fractures right thigh bone while walking outdoors with his mother; doctors diagnose an incurable bone disease as the cause of his fractures and stunted growth

1879–81   Makes frequent visits to mineral springs and spas in southern France with the hope of curing his condition; studies drawing and painting under René Princeteau, a friend of his father who was an animal painter

1882   Goes to Paris to apprentice at the studio of portrait artist Léon Bonnat

1883   Begins apprenticeship under Fernand Cormon, another successful painter; Countess Adèle buys Château de Malromé near Bordeaux, where Lautrec spends the summer

1884   Resides with René and Lily Grenier in their Montmartre apartment; begins trading his conservative lifestyle for a bohemian one

1885   Meets Impressionist painter Edgar Degas, whom he had long admired; begins frequenting Le Mirliton, Aristide Bruant's cabaret, and also exhibits his work there; has romantic relationship with Suzanne Valadon

1886   Leaves Cormon's atelier and rents his own studio at the corner of rue Caulaincourt and rue Tourlaque; exhibits under the pseudonym Tolau-Segroeg at the Salon des Incohérents

1887   Shares an apartment with Dr. Bourges in the same building where the Greniers live

1888   Exhibits at the Groupe des XX in Brussels where his work is critically acclaimed; Vincent van Gogh's brother, Théo, buys several of Lautrec's works for his gallery

1889   From this date on, exhibits almost every year at the Salon des Indépendents and the Cercle Volney in Paris; frequents the Moulin Rouge nightclub where he sketches the performers

1891   Receives a commission to make a poster for the Moulin Rouge; the daring style and innovative technique of the final work create a stir in the Paris art world

1892   Executes several successful lithographic posters, including those of Jane Avril, La Goulue, and Aristide Bruant; illustrates for Paris newspapers and magazines

1893   First major exhibition in Paris at the Goupil Gallery; moves in with his mother on rue de Douai in Montmartre

1894   Publishes lithographic album on Yvette Guilbert; visits London with Maurice Joyant; for three years resides on occasion in Paris brothels

1895   Befriends Thadée and Misia Natanson and illustrates for their newspaper; has growing fascination for both the theater and opera

1896   Exhibits at Joyant's Paris gallery; album of colored lithographs, *Elles,* is published; designs a poster for the Simpson bicycle chain; takes extended vacations in an attempt to quit his drinking habit

1897   Moves to a studio on rue Frochot; health declines rapidly; vacations at the seashore with various friends and seldom paints

1898   Exhibits in London where his work is criticized for its subject matter; illustrates *Histoires Naturelles* for Jules Renard; is increasingly paranoid due to overconsumption of alcohol

1899   Admitted to a mental hospital in Neuilly for detoxification treatment; is released after three months and placed in the care of a chaperon, Paul Viaud; resumes painting

1900   Designs programs for the opera; travels to Bordeaux where he rents an apartment and frequents the theater; has some paralysis in his legs but recovers

1901   Remains physically weak; returns to Paris to put his work in order; a stroke permanently paralyzes half of his body; his mother cares for him at her estate at Malromé; Lautrec dies on September 15, two months before his 37th birthday

INDEX

PICTURE CREDITS

The Art Institute of Chicago: p. 67; The Bettmann Archive: pp. 12, 80; Bibliothèque Nationale, Paris: pp. 16, 25; Bridgeman/Art Resource: p. 72; S.A. Denio Collection, and General Income, Courtesy Museum of Fine Arts, Boston: p. 92; Giraudon/Art Resource, NY: pp. 2, 19, 33, 36, 60, 65, 68, 69, 70, 74–75, 85, 88, 91, 94, 98, 102, 116, 121; Lauros-Giraudon/Art Resource, NY: pp. 44, 52, 97, 110, 113, 114; Erich Lessing/Art Resource, NY: pp. 70–71; Musée Toulouse-Lautrec, Albi, France: pp. 22, 26, 28, 31, 41, 48, 54, 57, 105; Museum of Modern Art, New York: p. 66; Roger-Viollet, Paris: pp. 15, 73, 106; Scala/Art Resource, NY: pp. 77, 94.

Jennifer Fisher Bryant is a freelance writer who specializes in biographies and has written 12 books, including *Louis Braille* in the Chelsea House GREAT ACHIEVERS series; *Marjory Stoneman Douglas: Voice of the Everglades*; and *Margaret Murie: A Wilderness Life*. A former high school teacher of French and German, Bryant holds a bachelor of arts degree in French and Secondary Education from Gettysburg College. She lives in Glenmoore, Pennsylvania, with her husband and daughter.

ACKNOWLEDGMENTS
The author wishes to thank Mr. Joseph Rishel, curator at the Philadelphia Museum of Art in Philadelphia, Pennsylvania, and Mr. Philip Rosenfeld, director at the Pennsylvania Art Conservatory in Berwyn, Pennsylvania, for their special contributions to this book. The author dedicates this book to Neil and Leigh.

Jerry Lewis is the National Chairman of the Muscular Dystrophy Association (MDA) and host of the MDA Labor Day Telethon. An internationally acclaimed comedian, Lewis began his entertainment career in New York and then performed in a comedy team with singer and actor Dean Martin from 1946 to 1956. Lewis has appeared in many films— including *The Delicate Delinquent, Rock a Bye Baby, The Bellboy, Cinderfella, The Nutty Professor, The Disorderly Orderly,* and *The King of Comedy*—and his comedy perfor- mances continue to delight audiences around the world.

John Callahan is a nationally syndicated cartoonist and the author of an illustrated autobiography, *Don't Worry, He Won't Get Far on Foot.* He has also produced three cartoon collections: *Do Not Disturb Any Further, Digesting the Child Within,* and *Do What He Says! He's Crazy!!!* He has recently been the subject of feature articles in the *New York Times Magazine,* the *Los Angeles Times Magazine,* and the Cleveland *Plain Dealer,* and has been profiled on "60 Minutes." Callahan resides in Portland, Oregon.